# The New Philanthropis

Charles Handy is a writer and broadcaster whose books have sold over one million copies in the UK. He is the author of *The Age of Unreason*, *The Empty Raincoat*, and *The Elephant and the Flea*, among other bestselling books. Elizabeth Handy is a portrait photographer whose work has been widely exhibited and published.

# The New Philanthropists

## THE NEW GENEROSITY

*Text by Charles Handy*
*Photography by Elizabeth Handy*

WILLIAM HEINEMANN: LONDON

Published by William Heinemann, 2007

1 3 5 7 9 10 8 6 4 2

Text copyright © Charles Handy, 2006

Photographs copyright © Elizabeth Handy, 2006

First published in the United Kingdom by William Heinemann, 2006

William Heinemann
Random House, 20 Vauxhall Bridge Road,
London SW1V 2SA

www.rbooks.co.uk

Addresses for companies within The Random House Group Limited can be found at:
www.randomhouse.co.uk

The Random House Group Limited Reg. No. 954009

A CIP catalogue record for this book
is available from the British Library

ISBN 978 0 434 017096

The Random House group Limited make every effort to ensure that the papers used in
its books are made from trees that have been legally sourced from well managed and
credibly certified forests. Our paper procurement policy can be found at:
www.randomhouse.co.uk/paper.htm

Typeset in Bembo MT by Palimpsest Book Production Limited,
Grangemouth, Stirlingshire
Printed and bound in Germany by Appl Druck, Wemding, Germany

# Contents

# Introduction

## The New Generosity

Generosity is fashionable again. The remarkable outpouring of donations from Britain and other rich nations after the tsunami catastrophe in South-east Asia in the final days of 2004 was just one very public example of a new attitude of compassion and generosity that seems to have developed in much of the wealthy developed world in recent years. *Time* magazine's choice of Bill and Melinda Gates along with Bono as the Persons of the Year in 2005 tuned into the mood of the times. *The Economist* followed suit, devoting a special survey to philanthropy in February 2006, and, later, coined the word 'philanthrocapitalism'.

As its author, Matthew Bishop, said, 'giving away money has never been so fashionable among the rich and famous.' He pointed out that the new fervour for giving was not confined to North America. In India the wealthy bosses of Infosys, Wipro and Dr Reddy's are joining more established business philanthropists such as the Tata, Birla and Bajas families, while in Latin America, Bishop quotes Martin Liechti of UBS as saying, whoever has become wealthy now has an agenda to give. In Russia, the oil magnate Roman Abramovich has given away millions to improve living conditions in Chukotka, where he is governor. Nor is Europe left out. In Germany, for example, the number of charitable foundations has trebled in the last ten years. Most notably, in June 2006 Warren Buffett, the world's second richest man, announced that he would give $31 billion of his hard-earned fortune to the Bill and Melinda Gates Foundation, effectively doubling its size.

America has long nurtured the tradition of 'giving back', in particular that those who have prospered should support the institutions from which they have benefited as well as helping those who will come after. Most of the giving in the past, therefore, went to religious organizations, to endowing scholarships or otherwise supporting their old school or college, or to funding the new wing of a hospital, a museum collection or an opera production. Robert Reich, writing in Stanford University's *Social Innovation Review*, said, 'we should stop kidding ourselves that charity and philanthropy do much to help the poor.'

The year 2005 was different, *Time* said. It was 'the year that redefined generosity, when America stirred itself awake from the dreamy indifference with which the world's poor had always been treated'. Katherine Fulton, the author of a recent report on the philanthropy industry, is also optimistic: 'if only 5-10 per cent of the new billionaires are imaginative in their giving, they will transform philanthropy over the next twenty years.'

Britain has always lagged behind in public generosity, donating just £226 per head per annum compared with America's £600. In 2003 the British, as individuals, gave £7.2 billion to charity, about the same as they spent on gambling that year, and just five per cent of the givers accounted for more than half of it. Legacies and charitable trusts added another £3 billion to the total. The reasons for Britain's relative parsimony are various. For example, in the past 100 years or so, there have been fewer seriously rich people than in the previous century, and the British tax regime has not historically looked as favourably on charitable gifts as its American counterpart. Thus, whereas much of America's charitable giving is planned, Britons contribute most of theirs through small donations, often collected on the street. Perhaps, too, the rise of the welfare state in Europe encouraged people to leave it to the state to look after the needs that weren't catered for by the market. 'I pay my taxes, don't I?' one tycoon responded when asked why he wasn't being more generous in his giving.

The British, along with most Europeans, have often traditionally preferred to give their time rather than their money. Roughly 26 million Britons, half the population, today volunteer their services to some good cause. Some do it more seriously than others. As an example of this sort of time philanthropist we met with Dr Daniel

McCloskey. On behalf of Afrimed, the medical charity that he helped to found, he gives all his free time to helping to identify surplus medical equipment in British hospitals that might be considered out of date in Britain but is still badly needed in Sudan. Afrimed, under his guidance, ships it to Sudanese hospitals, where Dr McCloskey supervises its installation, making three visits there a year in what are supposed to be his holidays. There are many such quiet volunteers in Britain, but time needs to be backed up with money to be truly effective.

There are now, however, some signs of change in Britain. Philanthropy is becoming fashionable. It is smarter today, Christine Odone of the *Observer*, commented, to be a do-gooder than a go-getter. Philip Beresford has added a Giving List to his *Sunday Times* Rich List. He has also noted that whereas in 1989 75 per cent of the giving came from inherited wealth and only 25 per cent was self-made, the position has now reversed, with seventy-five per cent coming from people who have made the money themselves. This was supported by the survey *Why Rich People Give* that Theresa Lloyd carried out for Philanthropy UK. She reported that 70 per cent of her interviewees were self-made, and half of that number were entrepreneurs, the other half professionals. Entrepreneurial Britain has been born again and is becoming generous. But these givers are different, they want to be involved, to initiate, not just respond. 'High engagement' is the fashionable phrase.

The new givers include, most obviously, international celebrities such as Bono and Bill and Melinda Gates, whose $31 billion foundation is the largest in history and is now due to double in size, or the Google duo, Sergey Brin and Larry Page, who have expressed the hope that their philanthropic arm will one day eclipse Google itself in overall world impact by 'ambitiously applying innovation and significant resources to the largest of the world's problems'. In Britain, Bob Geldof and Jamie Oliver have caught the public imagination. Individuals like these are proactive givers who apply to their social causes the skills and talents that made them successful.

Bill Gates takes the strategic foresight that he used to build Microsoft and applies it to the projects of his foundation. As Bono said, 'When Bill says you can fix malaria in ten years, you know he's done a few spreadsheets.' As musicians, Bono and Geldof have both mastered the skill of mass presentation. They have been able to focus the attention of the world on their concerns in a way that few others could. Nor have they been shy to use their celebrity status to gain access to the world's most powerful people, whom they need to back up their advocacy with action. Jamie Oliver was not content to bask in his success as a young, cocky TV chef and author. He wanted to do more with his talents and some of his money. He stirred the nation's and the British government's conscience with his TV programmes about school meals, proving that it was economically viable to provide healthy meals that children liked. His restaurant, Fifteen, has demonstrated that it is possible to take unemployed youngsters and turn them into professional chefs. Again, he had the confidence to display the process on television and to fund most of it with £1.3 million of his own money.

## British Philanthropists

My wife Elizabeth and I decided to investigate whether these high-profile entrepreneurial philanthropists were the visible signs of something wider and bigger. Were there others like them, below the radar of media attention? Were they only to be found in the United States or was the new approach more global? We wondered what the new rich in Britain are doing with their money, now that more people are becoming seriously wealthy in their early or midlife through their own efforts.

We knew that there were already a number of conspicuous and active givers in Britain. Lord David Sainsbury is one of the most generous. He established the Gatsby Charitable Foundation in 1967 with his inheritance, as just one of nineteen family trusts set up by the different members of that family. He recently announced that he intended to be the first Briton to give away £1 billion in his lifetime and will instruct the trustees of the Gatsby foundation to spend both the capital and the income before he dies. The Rausing family, who made their money from Tetra Pak, are also known for their often innovative benevolence.

There are many others. Sir Richard Branson has recently established the Virgin Foundation and announced that he intends to spend half of his time in future earning money for the foundation through his Virgin enterprises and half of his time working on social issues. Peter Simon of the fashion retailer Monsoon set up his foundation in 1994 to mark his company's twenty-fifth anniversary with the aim of supporting education for children and young women in India, where most Monsoon's products are made. In fact, more and more of the newly rich have established their own trusts or foundations, partly for tax reasons but also as a way to focus their giving. Men like Sir Tom Farmer, Michael Oglesby or Sir Robert Ogden channel their generous grant-giving to the needs of their regions. Half of the seventy-six high-net-worth individuals whom Theresa Lloyd interviewed for *Why Rich People Give* in 2005 had done just that. But, although many of the grants made by these trusts support new ventures, they were not the entrepreneurial pioneers that we were looking for.

Whether pioneers or not, individuals have been noticeably less shy in recent years to reveal their generosity. Vartan Gregorian, who runs the grant-making Carnegie Corporation of New York, would be pleased. 'I like people to be public about their generosity; it makes it more competitive if we can see who is doing what.' It also helps to encourage others. Anita Roddick, for instance, went on the BBC to declare her gift of £1 million to Amnesty International in which she is actively involved and has gone on to say that she intends to give away £50 million in the years ahead. She says that she publicized her Amnesty donation specifically in order to encourage others to act generously. It is well known that Sir Elton John has funded over 900 HIV/AIDS projects through his Aids Foundation, giving over £19 million in 2004 alone. David Gilmour of rock group Pink Floyd was not shy to let it be known that he gave the £3.6 million proceeds from the sale of his house to Crisis, to set up a community for homeless people.

Sports stars have been generous, too, and are not coy about it. Niall Quinn, the Sunderland and Irish footballer, gave the money from his testimonial match to various children's charities, and Martin Johnson, the England rugby captain, gave his testimonial gift to cancer charities. Nonetheless, Cathy Pharoah of the Charities Aid Foundation has estimated that the thirty top givers in the *Sunday Times* Giving List contributed only 1.2 per cent of their annual wealth, compared with the very wealthiest Americans who give as much as 13 per cent. There is still a lot of untapped potential for generosity.

Recognizing this, leading private bank Coutts has established a Family Business and Philanthropy Department to help private clients create their own strategies for effective giving. The bank's aim is to help its clients better understand the different ways of giving, so that they might make a bigger impact with their money and derive more personal satisfaction from the process. The bank organizes a rolling programme of philanthropy forums around the country where people can exchange views and experiences with other philanthropists as well as learn from selected advisers. In 2005 the bank was voted 'Best Provider of Philanthropy Services' by *Euromoney* magazine in recognition of its pioneering role. Other private banks and law firms are now following its lead, offering to provide advice to those with surplus funds but little idea of how to deploy them usefully.

They are not alone. In Britain, we discovered a new cluster of organizations with 'Philanthropy' in their titles, some of them dedicated to research and information on the sector, such as Philanthropy UK and the Institute for Philanthropy while others actively promote strategic investment in good causes, all indications of a rising interest in deliberate generosity. The UK Treasury, not wanting to be left behind, has recently created an Office of Charity and Third Sector Finance to coordinate policy on charitable giving. New Philanthropy Capital was established by a number of ex-bankers who decided to use their expertise to research what might best be called the markets for philanthropy, advising would-be givers where the needs are and how they can be met.

Venture philanthropy, or, more accurately, venture grant-making, is another idea borrowed from the private capital market but offering social rather than financial returns to its investors. It implies a long-term relationship with the chosen charity, providing hands-on support as well as funds. There are now some half a dozen venture philanthropy funds in Britain, supported by foundations and private investors, each providing long-term loans or grants to the causes the wealthy select. Venturesome is one of them. Launched in 2002 by the Charities Aid Foundation, it has invested around £6 million in over ninety charities, working with the recipients to ensure that the money is used appropriately. There are also rich people's clubs where the wealthy band together in order to focus their giving more effectively, and to spur others to contribute. The Network for Social Change is one example, as is the Serpentine Council, a private dining club with forty members. Ben Goldsmith's Manuka Club, whose members join together to support environmental causes is another. They are venture grant-giving trusts of a sort.

Among the venture grant-makers there are few organizations more effective in harnessing generosity than ARK (Absolute Return for Kids). Set up by a group of ex-bankers, its mission is 'to transform the lives of children who are victims of abuse, disability, illness and poverty' in the UK and other countries, such as South Africa. ARK's annual dinner in 2005 raised over £11 million in one night. Every £1 raised on the night was matched by an anonymous group of donors. A number of ARK's members are also, on their own account, each putting up the £2 million of capital required to create some of the government's proposed City Academies in or near London. Four are in the feasibility stage, with another four on the drawing board. They coordinate their efforts through ARK Education but are each personally involved in the schools that they sponsor.

Another innovative venture grant-maker is Dame Stephanie Shirley, an early entrepreneur in business technology who founded FI, now Xansa, in 1962. She went on to set up the Kingswood Trust for her autistic son and others like him and has since invested a total of £50 million in thirty projects in IT (her professional discipline) and autism. Her philanthropy, she says, is always pioneering and strategic.

This is not, however, the place for a detailed survey of Britain's philanthropic scene. That has been well done elsewhere, including Matthew Bishop's comprehensive *Economist* survey, Theresa Lloyd's Philanthropy UK report *Why Rich People Give*, based on anonymous interviews with a large sample of wealthy givers, and *The Guide to Giving*, also published by Philanthropy UK and supported by

Coutts Bank. These examples provide a taste of the new enthusiasm for giving that seems to have infected many of the seriously rich in Britain today. What we were still missing, however, were more examples of the kind of entrepreneurial philanthropy exhibited by the likes of Bill Gates and Jamie Oliver, individuals who took the initiative, who were still leading busy lives but used their know-how as well as their money to get something new off the ground, who did not invest in other people's projects but started their own. Ideally, they would be what some described as 'catalytic philanthropists', making an intervention that spurred on action by others. We went looking for them and found more than we expected.

# The Origins of this Book

With the encouragement of our publishers, we then decided to embark on this book with two aims: to celebrate the work and achievements of some of these 'New Philanthropists' and, crucially, to encourage other successful people to follow their example. We believe that social change is often triggered when new role models begin to set a new fashion. For that to happen these new heroes have to be individuals with whom others can identify. Their personal stories should excite the imagination. They must also be willing to put their heads above the parapet so that others can see them. We are very grateful to all those who allowed themselves to be both photographed and profiled. They did so, often reluctantly, because they agreed with us that there should be more like them.

The inevitable first questions are: who are these New Philanthropists, why are they new, and what is it that they have done that deserves celebration? The best way to find answers to these questions is to read their individual stories, but a short summary may help.

They are individuals, still in the prime of life, who have been successful in their chosen careers, made money, sometimes a lot of it, either in business or in their profession. Having made enough for their own needs they now want to use their money, their skills and their abilities to get things done to create something transparently useful in society. They talk of making a difference, of giving something back, but they aren't satisfied by writing cheques to worthy causes, valuable though such charity can be. These people want to be in the driving seat, because that's where they belong and, being by nature entrepreneurs of one sort or another, they like to fill gaps and to meet needs neglected by others. There is a feeling now in Britain that there are niches that the government can't or isn't filling; that if you have talent, energy and money you should move into these gaps and show the way. 'The chance to do this,' one interviewee said, 'makes the whole business of making money worthwhile.'

We need new words. Some shudder at the very word 'philanthropy', feeling it still carries overtones of Victorian *noblesse oblige*, of paternalistic and interfering do-gooding.

'Please don't call me a philanthropist, I am just trying to be useful,' one of them said. Others, such as Tom Hunter, like to describe themselves as venture philanthropists. They are true 'social entrepreneurs', but unlike most such people, they don't have to spend their time trying to raise the funds for their initial investments. They can write themselves a cheque without having to ask anyone else.

Philanthropy has almost become the new status symbol. To have your own foundation or a wing of a building named after you can be an outward and respectable mark of success. We should not sneer. If status is measured by how much one gives to others, society is the richer. But our new philanthropists are not driven by a desire for status. They required a lot of persuading to be featured in this book, lest they be thought to be parading their wealth or their good works. The best philanthropy, we were constantly told, was anonymous. The New Philanthropists featured here do what they do because they care and because they know how to make things happen. That is what their success is built on.

They are 'new' philanthropists because they don't fit the old mould of grant-giving foundations, responding to requests and applications. They are hands-on, pioneering and entrepreneurial, their resources dedicated to their own causes. They are new because they are still in the prime of life, with goals still to achieve, passions to satisfy, and the energy that is needed to start something new. Not for them any idea of what one termed 'post-mortem philanthropy' – they want to use their money while they are around to see the results. They are new because, since the end of the Victorian age, Britain has not until recently, with rare exceptions such as the Sainsbury family, had an entrepreneurial class capable of growing a business that would in time generate substantial wealth. The salaried clan of the large organizations and the public sector that have been the mainstay of British life for most of the past century never accumulated enough wealth to be able to make sizeable endowments, however charitably inclined they might have been. Only lately have the salaries and bonuses of some professionals been sufficiently big to create large disposable surpluses.

The example of these New Philanthropists is important. Not only does their entrepreneurial flair enrich the whole area of social enterprise but, by using the money that they made by their business acumen to improve the lot of others, they provide a social justification for the free enterprise system that it has often lacked. People should be judged, many of them feel, not only by how they made their money, but, as importantly, by how they spend it. These individuals spend it well, on purposes and causes beyond themselves, and they enjoy doing so. As Dr Frederick Mulder, an art dealer and the founder of the Funding Network, has said, 'using my profits to fund what I believe in is immensely satisfying.'

Not everyone likes the New Philanthropists, however, or what they do. Some accuse them of jumping into situations without doing enough research or of not understanding the longer-term implications of their initiatives. They can cross swords with established charities that have been working in the same areas for longer and resent the intrusions of the newcomers. In their efforts to get things moving the New Philanthropists can ruffle bureaucratic feathers, short-circuit procedures by going over the heads of local officials, or draw unwelcome publicity to faults in the system. As Geoff Mulgan, the director of the Young Foundation, has pointed out, profound social change does not come from a few inspiring projects or individuals. It generally needs a host of interlocking shifts in attitudes, social movements and markets, as well as involvement by government. But the change has to start somewhere and those whom we interviewed would claim that they are well aware of the pitfalls and do their best to work with others in the field as well as with the relevant authorities. If their initiatives are to have a lasting effect, they realize, they must eventually be integrated into the bigger system. Leverage is all, they say.

## How We Went About It

We looked for a representative sample of some twenty of these new heroes and ended up with twenty-three. We scoured newspapers, journals and reference works and consulted widely to find our exemplars. In order to demonstrate the broad scope for philanthropy we looked for variety in our sample – for different sizes of project working in different areas of need. We looked for campaigners as well as providers, for initiatives in the arts as well as in poverty, in housing as well as in education. It was important, we felt, to show how these newcomers to philanthropy went about creating their initiatives. No two were ever quite the same. Over half of them are British but, in order to demonstrate that this form of philanthropy is worldwide we also included an American, two Australians, a New Zealander, a Brazilian, a Sudanese, a Dutchman, a Slovenian and an Irishman. Their philanthropic contributions range from the many millions of Jeff Skoll, co-founder of eBay, or that Tom Hunter put into his foundation, to the £450,000 that Sara Davenport got from selling her art business to create the Breast Cancer Haven, the £60,000 of royalties that footballer Tony Adams received for his autobiography and used to start his Sporting Chance Clinic, or the £25,000 that Peter Ryan took from his salary to start a micro-loan operation in Malawi. You don't have to be a multimillionaire to be a New Philanthropist. The key is to have enough to be able to kick-start the enterprise without going begging. That way things can happen faster.

We sought to cover a variety of good causes. Education was an important one. In Scotland and now, allied with Bill Clinton, in Africa, Tom Hunter is seeking to grow a more entrepreneurial, self-responsible culture, as is Tony Falkenstein in New Zealand, or Brazil where Ricardo Semler is applying the principles of his norm-breaking business Semco to two schools in São Paulo, or back in Britain where Peter Lampl's Sutton Trust is breaking down the educational apartheid that he feels is blighting our future.

In other areas, Niall Mellon, an Irish a property developer, is building houses in the townships of South Africa with planeloads of Irish volunteers. David Ross, co-founder of Carphone Warehouse, has created an opera festival in middle England, while Janez Škrabec in Slovenia has single-handledly founded the Slovenian equivalent of English Heritage. Chris Mathias sends container-loads of second-hand computers to Africa while Jeff Gambin, a one-time restaurateur in Sydney, now pays for, distributes and helps to cook 400 meals a night for the homeless.

Bankers and ex-bankers feature on the list. John Studzinski supports young artists and composers, playwrights and directors through his Genesis Foundation. Ex-banker David Charters co-founded the Beacon Awards that celebrate social entrepreneurs and philanthropists, while Christopher and Phillida Purvis, ex-banker and ex-diplomat respectively, are now developing a centre in London to promote Japanese culture.

And so the list goes on. Ram Gidoomal retired at forty from his family business to become the inventive and imaginative creator of a unique variety of one-off charitable ventures in Britain, each designed to involve young people in the problems of the developing world. Carolyn Hayman left investment banking to become director and co-founder of Peace Direct, which provides support to peace activists in the danger points of the world. Mo Ibrahim, the pioneering genius behind the first mobile phones and now the chairman of Celtel in Africa, is building a breast cancer care centre in Khartoum, but his foundation is also investing in entrepreneurial new businesses in sub-Saharan Africa, with any profit returning to his foundation for reinvestment.

Gordon Roddick, lately of the Body Shop, invests in and oversees a range of social businesses, such as the Big Issue and Freeplay, operations with a social purpose that are intended to pay their own way, while Daniel Petre, ex-Microsoft, as well as having a well-focused venture grant-making foundation in Australia, spends much of his time and money campaigning for a better work–life balance in that country.

Tony Adams, footballing hero to many but also, in his past, an alcoholic, set up a clinic to help sports people with addictive problems and to begin to prepare the next generation of players for the challenges they will face. Most intriguingly, Jeff Skoll, in addition to supporting and promoting social entrepreneurs through his Skoll Foundation, has embarked on a personal mission to sponsor and underwrite major Hollywood films that raise issues of social justice or moral concerns. Two of these, *Syriana* and *Good Night, and Good Luck*, were box-office successes.

Entrepreneurial philanthropy, it is clear, can take several forms. There are many gaps that governments don't see or can't fill, many areas where the market doesn't work. New Philanthropists like the gaps: they offer opportunity for action. There could have been even more exemplar individuals. As our search progressed we were made aware of others whom it would have been a pleasure to have included, had time and space allowed. We hope, however, that the variety of individuals and causes is enough to allow those who are considering what to do with their money and energies 'beyond success' to find some person or cause with which they can identify and which will spur them into doing likewise.

## The Interviews

Having identified and tracked down our subjects we first had to meet them to get their agreement. They needed to understand our motives and to be reassured as to our credentials. It helped, perhaps, that Elizabeth and I had previously written a similar book together, called *The New Alchemists*, which had been a publishing success.

We told them that Elizabeth, a professional portrait photographer, would want to photograph them in as natural a way as possible. She also asked them if they would agree to prepare a still life with her, for which they would choose five objects and one flower that would symbolize what was most important to them in their lives. She would then arrange the objects and photograph them so that the resulting still life would be a pictorial representation of their life and values. Our thinking was that this would help both us and the reader better to understand the person behind the achievements.

People were often very imaginative in their choice of symbolic objects. One man included a pile of poker chips and a bottle of champagne. These, he explained, were nothing to do with a love of either gambling or drink. The poker chips reminded him that a degree of risk was essential in any entrepreneurial venture, philanthropic or otherwise. If there were no risk, the limit had not been reached. And the champagne?

Any worthwhile job well done needed to be celebrated, with the other people involved, and there would always be others, because nothing of any note can be accomplished alone. Another included a pencil in his still life because, he said, nothing is irreversible, anything can be rubbed out and redone. The flower he chose was a sunflower because it is always looking for the light. More personal still was the choice by another of a hand-dynamo torch. 'That light is like love. You have to work at it to keep it alive.' These comments and others like them are captured in the interviews. The still lives are another way of looking at each individual, an alternative portrait.

## The Similarities

The twenty-three individuals and their projects are, by design, very different. Some are shy, others extrovert. Some are driven by spiritual or religious feelings, others by a sense of social responsibility or just a need to help and be useful. What they all have in common, however, can be summed up in three words – Passion, Permanence and Partnership.

No entrepreneurial venture will succeed without a large injection of energy and personal commitment. Good ideas, even carefully researched business plans, are not enough in themselves. Given passion, however, any problems can be dealt with, any difficulty endured. Niall Mellon would not fly out from Dublin to South Africa twice a month if he was not passionately committed to his township project. Jeff Gambin could not give up his lifestyle to feed

400 homeless people every night unless he was passionate about it. Peter Lampl would not give most of his time and a lot of his money to his educational trust unless he was passionate about ending what he sees as educational apartheid in Britain. That was true of all of them. What they do is not required of them, is not done for status and certainly not for personal gain. They do it because it is what they believe in.

The passion is often triggered by some event. Peter Lampl recalls how he woke up one day to find himself on the front page of *The Times* for a charitable initiative and realized that one person can make a difference to the way things are done. David Charters discovered one weekend that his immersion in his work had lost him his family and resolved to change his life. Christopher Purvis calculated on the back of an envelope one evening that he had enough money to meet all his family's needs for the foreseeable future and decided there and then to change his life. Sara Davenport's nanny's poor treatment for breast cancer stung Sara into doing something about it, even when that meant selling her treasured business. Ram Gidoomal had an eye-opening experience in Mumbai that forced him to look again at his priorities.

Tom Hunter took a phone call one morning offering to buy his business for a sum that would take care of all his future financial needs and set about deciding how he wanted to use the rest of his life. He was only thirty-seven. Others, like Jeff Skoll, Michael de Giorgio and Chris Mathias, had similar experiences, when they sold their businesses. They were all fortunate in that they were able to find projects that consumed their interest and allowed them to turn an unexpected opportunity or problem into a passion. Had that not happened, one suspects, they would have been content to set up a family trust or foundation and just respond to requests for assistance. There would be nothing wrong with that, and many have done it, but they would not then have initiated the projects that they did. To be the kind of catalysts that they hoped to be, there had to be passion and the commitment that comes from that.

The New Philanthropists have all been successful, most of them in business, and many still retain some business interests. They look at their philanthropic projects in a businesslike way and see their interventions as an initial investment of money, time and energy, but they are clear that their projects have to be self-sustaining in the long run. In the end their initiatives have to stand on their own. If they can't, the founders themselves would be trapped into a continuing role as principal supporters and funders, leaving them unable to move on to other projects. If the investment of their time and energy is to make a real difference, it has to last beyond their own graves; it has to have a permanent impact.

Some of them are careful to build in alternative sources of support. Jeff Gambin has started a new for-profit enterprise in Sydney, specifically to earn enough money to fund his project when his own money runs out or he departs. Mo Ibrahim's breast cancer clinic in Khartoum will be seven storeys high, but the top two storeys will be let out as luxurious office suites, the income from which will support the clinic in future years. Gordon Roddick insists that the social businesses in which he invests his money and time break even after a specified period and, he says, he keeps a close eye on them to make sure they meet his targets.

Sustainability, however, ultimately depends on partnership of one sort or another. Others must have a continuing interest in the projects or else they will tend to die when the original sponsor and investor moves on. If new projects are to be more than an interesting experiment, they need to be scaled up. That often requires a partnership between fleas and elephants. Fleas, be they individuals or tiny groups, can be more creative and experimental but they need larger organizations or movements, the elephants, to roll out the results. The track record of elephants for innovation, in any field, has not been good. Fleas, on the other hand, can do little on their own. The poor record Britain has acquired for the development of new ideas in business is largely due to the lack of these sorts of partnerships between the inventive fleas and the efficient and resource-rich elephants. The best of the New Philanthropists know this.

Peter Lampl organized and funded the first summer school at Oxford University but was careful to involve not only the university but also David Blunkett, then the Secretary of State for Education, with the result that there are now summer schools at sixty universities, jointly run by the universities and the Department for Education. He has said that 'where a project has proven its efficacy, we work closely with government to secure nationwide uptake and funding'. Tom Hunter is delighted that his investment of £35 million in education in Scotland has leveraged £175 million of government spending, extending his pilot schemes across the country.

Niall Mellon could not hope to make more than a small dent in the housing problem of South Africa without the help and involvement of the local municipalities and the national government. They had to fund and prepare the infrastructure on the sites, validate the leases and subsidize part of the price of the houses he built. The volunteers whom he flies out from Ireland are also partners in that they all raise money to pay for their own fares and accommodation and contribute to the cost of the houses. Partnership creates involvement, which builds commitment and long-term sustainability.

Peter Ryan provided the initial investment for his micro-loan operation in Malawi but has been careful to share the overall supervision with members of his local church community and to involve the British government as a co-funder once the project was off the ground. Tony Falkenstein's investments in entrepreneurial education necessarily involved the cooperation of the schools and universities involved, but he has also striven to make them dependent upon complementary help from government. Leverage is always key.

We would like to think that the examples of these New Philanthropists will also have an indirect leverage; that their example will inspire others, even if they and we never know of it. We believe that there is an increasing number of successful professionals and entrepreneurs in our society who must sometimes wonder what they should do 'beyond success'. We hope that the stories of the individuals in this book will have given them some ideas, and some encouragement.

Charles and Elizabeth Handy
Norfolk and London, 2006

# Tony Adams

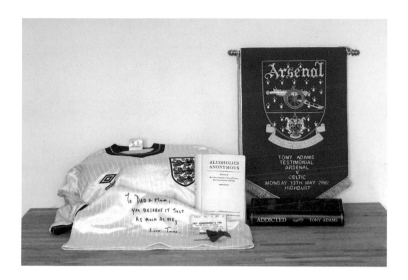

At 5.00 p.m. on Friday 16 August 1996 Tony Adams had what, God willing, he says, will be his last drink of alcohol. He was twenty-nine years old and an English football hero, the captain of Arsenal and England, but also, as he finally admitted to himself, an alcoholic.

It had been a star-studded career thus far – at seventeen he had played his first match for the Arsenal first team. Three years later he played his first game for England and a year later, on New Year's Day 1981, he became the youngest ever captain of Arsenal, one of England's leading clubs, going on to captain his country six years later. By then he was also married with three children.

It had not, however, been trouble-free. A spell in prison for drink-driving should have sobered him up, but it didn't. So should falling down a nightclub steps, cutting his head and needing twenty-nine stitches. So should a long sequence of embarrassing incidents, all chronicled with meticulous honesty in his book, *Addicted*.

With that final drink he had, he realized, reached the bottom. After a long weekend of hot sweats and shivers, dehydration and a lot of tears, he pulled himself together enough to make it to training with his team. 'What had been an athlete's 29-year old body a couple of months ago,' he says, 'felt more like a 60-year-old man's as I stumbled across the car park, where – and it was surely meant to be – I bumped into Steve Jacobs,' a friend of footballer Paul Merson's, who had been helping Paul recover from his addictions. 'I've got a drink problem and I need to go to a meeting of Alcoholics Anonymous,' Tony blurted out. It was the first time he had asked another person for help, and it was to be the start of his recovery.

He went on to lead his club to that rare feat, the double triumph of winning both the Premier League Championship and the FA Cup, in 1998, and to be honoured by the Queen with an MBE in 1999. By the time he retired in 2002 he had played in over 500 league matches and had appeared 66 times for England, captaining them 15 times. He was resolved, however, as a result of his own earlier problems to do what he could to help the next generation of professional players to cope better with the pressures of a career that starts in one's teens and lasts, on average, for only six years, and of a life that is often lived in the public eye, under the scrutiny of the press.

'I was getting all these phone calls from footballers, lots of requests, not so much for advice, but to share my experience, how did I get help, what worked for me. It was taking up a lot of my time. There was a need here, I could see.' He considered setting up a foundation to give grants to existing treatment centres but he felt that there was a demand for a facility specially focused on athletes, one that would take account of their physical needs as well as their emotional problems. It was then that he happened to read a column about charities in a Sunday paper by Ros Harwood, who was on the point of leaving the Charity Commission to set up her own office in York. 'That's it, I thought, I'll set up a charity and see if I can get her involved.'

In 2000 he set up the Sporting Chance Clinic with the proceeds of his book, around £60,000, after first commissioing a survey by a couple of American experts on the current situation in the English football scene. Later he added the money raised by his testimonial match, another £160,000 or so; 'I'm not sure of the exact sums, I was writing cheques all over the place at the time just to get it up and running. But that's it,' he now says, 'it has to stand on its own legs from now on.' And it does. In 2002 he appointed Peter Kay as CEO. Peter had been a highly acclaimed professional chef, working in Michelin-starred restaurants and hotels, but had had his own addiction problems with alcohol and other drugs. He, too, had sought help from Alcoholics Anonymous and had become a close friend in 1996 when Tony was going through his own recovery. Peter had gone on to put together his own seminar on alcohol and other drug awareness and become a recognized expert on the subject.

The Sporting Chance Clinic is small by design, with only four-teen full-time staff. 'Small works better, I find,' says Tony, but the clinic has big ambitions. It has three components, Tony explains, 'before, during and after'. Its first priority is education – at every level. 'Education is expensive, but it's key.' Staff go into schools and clubs. 'The Football Association back that. The Scottish FA gives a little. The Jockeys Association gave us ten grand.' Footballers are not the only atheletes to have addiction problems. The educational events concentrate on sharing experiences, but they also work on life skills and on the challenges of life after professional sport, given that Tony's own twenty-year career in football is the exception. The 90 per cent of footballers who have left the game by the age of twenty-one will not have received much education between the ages of thirteen and nineteen.

The second leg of the charity's work is residential, at Liphook, Hampshire, in the grounds of a health farm. Staff work with small groups on a 28-day residential programme. The treatment side is run by James West who was Tony's own therapist. Indeed, all the work of the clinic, as Peter Kay, the chief executive, explains, is based on Tony's own experience. Whenever possible, Tony will have lunch with the residents of the clinic, reassuring them, just by his presence, that there is a way ahead. He is, Peter Kay says, the living example of how one can conquer addiction. 'If the Captain of England can be open about his problems, so can anyone.' Any seriously addicted individuals are referred to alcohol or drug clinics leaving the clinic free to work with those who have not yet reached the bottom. Some of these may be ex-footballers, for life after retiring from the game may be as stressful as the time within it. This is the 'after' aspect of the clinic's work. The clinic also acts as a halfway house for addicted footballers who have ended up in prison. They may have been helped to recover from their addiction in prison but still need to be better prepared for life on the outside.

The clinic charges people what they can afford for the treatment, bearing in mind that it is not the richer, more successful footballers that need help but, more usually, the ones who are struggling. The current charge is £350 a night (compared with higher-profile clinics, which typically charge £550 or more). There is also a pot to help those who need it. 'And, would you believe it, we have never turned anyone away,' Tony says.

It is the chief executive's job to balance the books, soliciting support from the clubs and the Associations. 'Someone has to take responsibility for these youngsters. The clubs only have them for a short time and then they are gone. It is organizations like the Rugby Football Union, the Professional Footballers' Association who need to be concerned.' The clinic can only make a small difference, although Peter Kay believes that its educational work has created a new awareness among footballers of the problems of drink. The hope must be that the professional bodies will follow the lead that Tony has given and take up where the clinic leaves off. Other bodies could help. In one instance the borough of Tower Hamlets contributed to a rehabilitation programme for a footballer who had ended up in prison. Tony himself is the founder trustee and chairs the quarterly meetings. He also is more than happy to go into schools to talk about his experiences. 'I enjoy that; but it's also part of my own recovery programme.'

For Tony himself, however, it is time to move on. 'I'm very proud of the charity but it must make its own way now.' He won't leave football, however. Football was, and probably always will be, the core of his life, along with his family. The items he chose for his still life bear witness to this, with pride of place going to his first England shirt and the pennant from his testimonial match at Arsenal at the end of his career. But beside them, smaller in size but not in importance, are the theatre ticket he bought for his first night out with Poppy, his wife, along with the Remembrance Day poppy as one more symbol of his love for her and his family. He wouldn't be who he is now, however, without Alcoholics Anonymous, and its 'Big Book' is his tribute to the people who 'saved my life', along with his own book that tells how his rescue came about.

As soon as Tony retired, he embarked on a research degree at Brunel University on youth development in football, while more broadly investigating what he calls the social anthropology of football. How is it, for instance, that a small country like Holland produces so many talented footballers, or that Brazil has 10,000 of them? Closer to home there were the issues with which the Sporting Chance Clinic is concerned – the development and education of athletes and their preparation for life after their playing days are over.

To back up his research he took on the management of a poorly performing club, Wycombe Wanderers, for a year. That turned out to be more of a challenge than he had bargained for. The club was losing £6,000 a week when he arrived and was bottom of League Divsion One. He had to let go nineteen out of twenty-eight players as soon as their contracts expired, but he then began to turn around both the club's fortunes and its finances. A year was enough, however, and he went on to spend six months coaching young players in France, Italy and Holland. He had, along the way, taken a course in Business Studies at Warwick Business School and had obtained the 'A' Licence from the UEFA, the key licence to coach professionally. It had been a busy three years since his retirement. He had also married again, was expecting a second child with his new wife, Poppy, and had moved to the country.

Fame can be a trap, Tony reflects. Your past won't let you go, making it difficult to move on. 'I had earlier realized that I would not be free until I had moved my problems into the public domain and made a clean breast of everything. Then the journalists and others would have nothing on me. All would be in the open.' And when things are right they seem to fall into place, he finds. So it was that, one day soon after the start of his recovery from alcoholism, he met Eddie Bell, the head of publishing company HarperCollins, who turned out to be an Arsenal supporter and who suggested he write a book. In the very same week he met Ian Ridley, a journalist and also a recovering alcoholic, who agreed to help him write it. They went off to the South of France where Tony mixed his training with long talks into a tape recorder. After that Ian worked on the chapters, sending each one to Tony for his comments. The whole process took some eighteen months, and the finished book ended up on the shortlist for the Sports Book of the Year.

Tony's life is still focused on football, but what his future role will be is not yet clear. It may be easier, he thinks, to work abroad, where his name is not so well known and the trap of fame not so tight. His record on the pitch obscures anything else he does or tries to do. The cavils as well as the plaudits still continue although his playing days are long since over. 'It can be cruel at times,' Peter Kay says. 'People just don't realize how much money and time and energy this man has put into this charity, and the good that it has done.' Tony himself, however, should have no doubt that he has made a huge difference to the sport he loves, by his example as much as by his philanthropy. As a result of what he had gone through, he saw a gap that needed to be filled and went ahead and filled it.

## Still Life

Tony's first England shirt – his sporting achievement
Arsenal testimonial pennant – his football club
Theatre ticket – love for his wife (first date together)
AA 'Big Book' – Alcoholics Anonymous
*Addicted* – his autobiography
Poppy – his wife and family

# David Charters

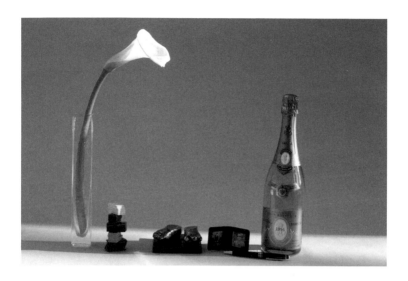

'In life you have to be prepared to take risks,' says David Charters. 'Life is a roulette game; we have the choice of where to place our chips. We have so many years given to us and, in theory, as you get older the chips you have to play with get more valuable, so the decisions therefore become more crucial.' In 2000, at the age of thirty-nine, David Charters took the riskiest decision of his life – he left his lucrative job in the City to start a new life, largely devoted to philanthropy.

Why did he do it? The City had just experienced two of its most buoyant years. At Deutsche Bank the bonuses had been bountiful, to say the least. 'I was lucky. They say that one should never confuse brains with a bull market and we had enjoyed the best bull market for many years.' His colleagues thought he was mad not to want more of the same. 'Just pass Go a few more times and you can relax,' as they put it. But he remembered something that another of those colleagues had said to him early on in his career there. Three things matter in life, he told David, the first and most important is family, then comes work because it takes up so much of your time, but the third is one that is often missed, the special interests that make you unique as a person.

David was only too aware that he had got the three things out of balance in recent years. Life on the trading floor of a merchant bank had been lucrative and fun but all-absorbing. After thirteen years there he had acquired a beautiful home in the country, complete with swimming pool, tennis court, lakes and plenty of land. He had four young children and a Porsche 911 for his wife. 'Materially, it was all wonderful, but I was on the road 168 days of the year. When I came home at weekends I was exhausted. With four demanding children I'm sure that I paid attention to them but that I was in some measure a neglectful husband and took things for granted that I shouldn't have. Then I found out that she was having an affair. It was the classic City divorce.'

That was in 1998. Two years later, back in London on his own again, he had piled up the money and taken another risk, having met, wooed and married Luisa to start a new family, resolved this time to get the priorities right. But what, then, were his special interests, what did he want to do with his one unrepeatable life?

The first answer was the Beacon Fellowship Charitable Trust. His idea was nothing less than to change the whole culture of giving in this country. Why not think big? The fellowship might itself be a small thing but it would be like casting a pebble into a pool. The fellowship would acknowledge and celebrate unusual philanthropists through a set of annual awards. The idea came from a conversation with a banking colleague, John McClaren, who introduced David to Emily Stonor, who had been head of communications at the Science Museum and is now the chief executive of the trust. Together they toured the country, raising support, promoting the idea, discussing it with focus groups, treating it, in fact, very like a traditional product launch. David has put in £300,000 of his own money to kick-start it but a lot more of his time and energy.

A large constituency of support needed to be created to maximize the number of nominations and to spread the idea. It took time, and much consultation with every interested party. The first prizes were awarded in 2003 in 11 Downing Street, hosted by the Chancellor of the Exchequer, Gordon Brown. There were over 700 nominations and thirteen prizes were awarded in six different categories with scope for the judges to award special prizes. The overall winner was given £20,000 to donate to a charity of their choice. This was the final outcome of the work of six trustees, seven judges, twenty-six scrutineers, ten members of the Founder Partners' Advisory Board and fourteen members of a General Advisory Board, not forgetting twenty-seven Benefactors and supporters, both individuals and companies. The accounts show a total expenditure of £1,260,000 for that first year. This was not a small undertaking.

The prizes celebrate the work of a wide range of philanthropists and social entrepreneurs, some well known such as Paul Getty (posthumously) or John Profumo, but also many unsung heroes such as David Constantine, who, left quadraplegic after a diving accident, co-founded Motivation, which designs and makes affordable wheelchairs for people in developing countries. Today, 15 years later, more than 25,000 people in 17 countries have benefited from the use of a Motivation wheelchair.

Using examples such as these, the Beacon Fellowship seeks to make it fashionable to change the culture of giving in the country. 'In Britain,' says David, 'charitable work is regarded as worthy but you keep quiet about it. That is a pity because some of the best ideas come from individuals no one hears about.' The fellowship therefore celebrates individuals who have transformed the lives of others, either by a single brilliant idea or by an act of courage or sustained dedication to an important cause. It seeks to reward inspirational, imaginative and sometimes downright obstinate people who never make it to the honours lists and don't always feature among the nation's movers and shakers.

For its work to succeed the fellowship needs wide support, public recognition and high-level encouragement. By all accounts it is succeeding. The extensive coverage of the first award ceremony in all the main papers was some proof of that recognition, as was the quality of the next set of nominations. An independent evaluation of the first year concluded that there was 'much admiration for the amount that Beacon has achieved in only one year'. If more of the shining examples of good practice can be persuaded to come forward, the longer-term aims of the fellowship will be met.

But David now plans to move on. Initiatives such as this need to become self-reliant, he maintains. 'You will only have succeeded if it survives after you have gone.' Initially, he was the chequebook of last resort, but after what will be two successful years he is no longer needed either as a chequebook or as chairman of the trustees and the judges. It is time for him to rebalance his life once again, giving more attention to his new business interests, which he had been neglecting during the build-up of the trust. He is a partner in a small investment bank that offers advice to companies, often in return for a share in the equity. Then there is his own wealth to manage, something that, given his entrepreneurial hands-on nature, naturally ends up involving him in the affairs of the enterprises in which he invests. These business interests inevitably and rightly feed into his charitable work. Part of the success of the Beacon Fellowship is undoubtedly due to the management and networking skills that David has brought to it from his business career. This is a man used to taking decisions, at ease with handling relationships and skilled at distinguishing the important from the trivial. Keeping these skills fine-tuned in the competitive world of business can only add to his effectiveness and credibility in the charitable world.

To add to his connections with the hard reality of life he is also a magistrate, a role that has aroused his interest in drug policy, which he feels is going in the wrong direction, while his own experience gives him a personal interest in the issues raised by the former campaign group Fathers for Justice. 'I was sitting as a magistrate in Bow Street the day two of them threw condoms of purple flour on to the floor of the House of Commons. One of them was fined £600. I thought that if I had imposed that fine, I would have been very tempted to say "And I would be delighted to pay it for you!"' But he now intends to focus most of his charitable energy on Action for Blind People. Oh, and he is also writing a novella about life in the City. So, yes, he is busy, as are most effective people, but, he says, he now has control of his own time and that makes all the difference.

He became a trustee of Action for Blind People last year and intends to get more actively involved as soon as he has left the Beacon Fellowship. The charity provides practical help for blind people, including ways to help them back to work, a housing advisory service and sheltered housing, holiday hotels, sports facilities and a general support service. 'In theory social services should be doing all this, but in practice they can't, so we do,' David explains.

Why this particular charity? 'It is my personal nightmare – going blind,' he says. Like most successful philanthropists, therefore, David Charters follows his heart. He exudes optimism, the sense that the world can be made better if decent people do something about it. His own life now is based at his home, surrounded by his family, his wife Luisa, their two young children and his son Mark from his first marriage. No longer is he the absentee husband and father, no longer is his work somewhat beyond his control, no longer is his life divided in two. 'I'm busy, but I can take the odd day off, walk Alexander to school, that sort of thing.' There should, David believes, always be room for a bit of champagne in life, to signify success and celebration, love and the sheer joy of living.

What drives him now, then? 'It all goes back to Mum and Dad. One of the things I'm always conscious of is that where you come from ultimately shapes how you carry on in life. They were great parents. We didn't have much money.' His father, he explains, was a Barnado's boy who won a place at the local grammar school but had to go into hospital for eighteen months and missed out on his place. When he came out he was told that he could be either a cobbler or a tailor. He chose the tailor. His mother was a shop assistant.

'They were, are, the classic good people who worked hard, raised their families and were very happy to sacrifice themselves to allow my sister and myself to make the most of our lives.' David went to grammar school, then to Cambridge where he got a First Class degree; he then joined the Foreign Office and, after a few years, went into the City with SG Warburg and, later, Deutsche Bank. 'At every stage my parents were delighted and pinching themselves and thinking this is fantastic. It's very easy in the City to lose touch with reality. They kept my feet on the ground.' His father, he feels, had a raw deal but has never borne a grudge, has always looked on the positive side, never complained. It is largely because of his parents that David feels that it is only right that, having been fortunate, he ought to try to give something back.

There is, he believes, an altruistic urge in all of us, as the Beacon Prizes demonstrate but it often needs a trigger to release it. For David it was undoubtedly his divorce that forced him to rethink his life. Painful though the experience was, and still is, it set him on the course and towards the rebalanced life that he now finds so fulfilling.

## *Still Life*

Photograph of David's parents – core values
Roulette chips, from Luisa's mother – risk and choice
Pen – banking and books
Bronze cast of Alexander's feet – family
Champagne – celebration, exuberance and success
Lily – love and Luisa

# Sara Davenport

The London Haven lives up to its name. Walk into it and you enter a true oasis of peace and goodness. You feel immediately welcomed and accepted. No one is judging you – a rare feeling in a busy world. It is the London branch of Breast Cancer Haven, founded in the late 1990s to provide support, companionship and therapy to those suffering from breast cancer. It was the first such place at the time, much needed and much welcomed. There is now another Haven in Hereford and more are planned when funds become available, all under the banner of Breast Cancer Haven. The charity owes its existence to a determined and enterprising young woman who sold her thriving art gallery to create the first Haven.

Sara was a young mother at the time. Wendy, the nanny of her children was unexpectedly diagnosed with breast cancer. Wendy was middle-aged, unsophisticated and baffled by much of the medical terminology. She had no idea what a mastectomy was nor did anyone explain to her what was involved. She would turn up for her appointment at the hospital only to find they had put her down for the wrong day. She never saw the same doctor twice and found the whole process confusing and distressing. 'At first I thought she was just unlucky,' said Sara, 'but then I began to meet a lot of other people who had the same sort of stories to tell. I was horrified. I knew that the NHS was hard-pressed but I could not believe that the system could be so chaotic and, well, uncaring. It is not just the physical body that needs attention but also the mental, emotional and the spiritual side of us, too.' Women in particular, she felt, need to talk to kindred spirits and have the chance to share their feelings and anxieties. Sara hastens to say that she does believe that the system is now much better than it was ten years ago.

'This is not good enough,' she said to herself and started investigating. She found that there were indeed lots of different forms of support for cancer sufferers but they were all in different places and under various names and organizations. 'When you are ill you do not have the energy to do the research, let alone find your way to all the different locations. I talked to the breast cancer charities, but most of them were concerned with research, which is great, but if I were ill I would want help now, not in the distant future. Breast Cancer Care runs a telephone helpline, but what I felt was needed was a place, a place where all the different forms of advice and help, apart from the physical treatment, were all under one roof and where you would have a chance to talk to others who could understand what you were going through.'

She went to talk to the existing charities. 'This is what is lacking,' she explained. They didn't agree. 'It's fine as it is,' they said. But it was not, she knew, fine as it was. By this time she had talked to literally hundreds of breast cancer sufferers, doctors and nurses who had all agreed that her idea of a 'haven' was what was needed. 'So I went back to the charities and said to them, "If I raise the money and give it to you will you do it?"' When they refused, saying it wasn't needed, she knew she would have to do it herself.

The only way she could do that would be to sell her art gallery. In her early twenties she had started a unique gallery that dealt only in nineteenth-century dog paintings, a very specific niche, for which she became known far and wide. It was, she said, a excellent little business. Everyone who wanted to sell or buy a nineteenth-century dog painting would find their way to her. If she had one to sell, she knew whom to approach. There was no time wasted in marketing to the general public. To sell the business after twelve years or so would be tough. 'I loved my gallery, loved my dog pictures, loved my clients – and I made lots of money. It was a terrible dilemma, but I knew that if I didn't do it I would always regret it. I could have gone on running the gallery until I was seventy-five, but I had done it, I knew how to do it, it wouldn't have got any different or any better.' It was time to change. But it wouldn't be easy, or quick, as she debated with herself the pros and cons of giving up what she knew and loved for something completely different.

When she told people what she intended they were universally discouraging. 'You knew everything about your subject in the art gallery,' they told her 'but you know nothing about breast cancer or running a charity. You couldn't even be the receptionist.' Sara was undaunted. 'No, of course I don't, but sometimes I think it is better not to be an expert because the people who do know what they are doing don't always know what is needed.' She added, 'When people say I can't do something it gets me irritated. Right then, I say to myself, I'm going to show them!' She tells how, when she was trying to set up her gallery, aged twenty-two, she approached her bank manager with what seemed a cast-iron business plan with references in support from all the leading gallery owners, and asked for an increase of £10,000 on the mortgage on her flat. The manager leaned across his desk and said, 'If you were a boy, Miss Davenport, I would give it to you, but you are a girl and therefore less reliable. You do see my dilemma.' 'What did you say?' exclaimed Sara, horrified, only to be stung into instant action. She quickly found another bank, another manager, got a loan for substantially more money and paid it off in eighteen months.

The actual sale of all her beloved paintings was emotionally difficult. Yet, she recalls, once the sale was over and all the paintings had gone, it was as if they had never been. A chapter had closed. 'I will never be frightened by change again,' she says. The sale of the paintings and the lease on the gallery raised about £450,000. She was ready to go, but to where?

'I believe very strongly,' Sara says, 'that when things are meant to happen they happen very easily. Doors open.' And so they did. She found herself sitting next to the manager of an oil company at an event. He asked her what she did, and she replied that she was starting a charity and was looking for space. He said that his company was moving their office to the country and wanted to loan the spare space to a charity. Could she come and pitch for it on Wednesday? She did and found herself, along with Rowena Bartlett, her ex-colleague at the art gallery and newly appointed CEO of the yet-to-be Haven, sitting in a posh office in St James's Square, along with a large board-room for meetings, computers in abundance and even the part-time services of a secretary, all for free. 'It gave us respectability. People took us seriously.' No longer were they a couple of women sitting in a basement looking for funds. They stayed there for two years, because, while the money from the gallery sale might have paid for a building it would have needed another million to do it up and to cover the running costs if, as they intended, their service was to be free of charge to all who needed it.

'It isn't easy to raise money when you only have an idea,' but Sara believes that the one essential to success is to be completely sure of where it is that you want to get to. How you get there will evolve. It took six months to find a building – in the end a decayed church in Fulham Broadway, then still a rather seedy area. 'It's very, very, very important to me,' says Sara emphatically, 'that the prem-ises have the right feeling, the right energy. I'm incredibly sensitive to that, and I know it when it's there. Sometimes when you walk into a hospital you know that terrible things happen in there – part of it is the architecture and the paint, but part is the pain that people are suffering – you can feel it.' Architects showed her many build-ings. She rejected them. The church had the right feeling, despite its appalling state. 'This is the one,' she insisted. No one else agreed. 'It's horrible,' they said. And it was, but not when she was finished with it.

It took a year to transform, 'with the help of some extraordinary people', many of them sourced from the Yellow Pages. Sara was initially petrified at the thought of cold-calling but, she found, 'people are often incredibly nice'. She recalls making a presentation to the manager of Furniture Village and asking him for any furniture he could spare. 'No, I'm sorry,' he said, and her face fell. 'I haven't finished,' he said, then went on, 'we will only take part on one condition – that we give you all the furniture for the entire building.' They opened in 2000 – after one small hiccup. When it was time to sign the building contract Sara had her misgivings after talking to the owner of the building firm, whom she had not met before, and refused to sign. 'I knew he wasn't right.' But doors do open for her. She went to dinner that night and when her neighbour at the table asked her what she did, she told him the story. 'Well,' he said, 'I'm a builder. I'll do it for you. When do you want us to start?' And he did it for less money.

They still had to raise the funds, but to do that they needed a board of trustees. 'I wasn't right for chairman. My talent is for starting things, not running them. I am just one of the trustees. We looked for people who were the best in their field. Everyone we approached was, of course, already an experienced businessman as well as a chairman or trustee of several other charities and didn't really want another, but they were all incredibly nice and agreed, especially our chairman, Jeremy Leigh Pemberton, who said he would do it for the first two years and was still there until very recently.'

Sara may be right that doors do open when the idea is right, but someone still has to turn the handle. Looking back, it seems clear that Sara brought to the Haven project the same kinds of skills that she had used at her gallery. These include her ability to sense a gap in the market that others have ignored and her talent with people, given that most chief executives don't immediately offer help to someone they meet over the dinner table. 'I'm very good at selling,' she admits, almost apologetically. And she is an eternal optimist. 'I'm the kind of person who will walk to the edge of a cliff and then walk over it because I expect to fly. Of course, sometimes I might break a leg but often one does fly.' These skills, when combined with the same sort of passion that she brought to her dog paintings as well as her readiness to trust her intuition even when everyone thinks her mistaken, have made her a formidable entrepreneur in both the business and the charity fields.

Having given away not only her business assets but also her main source of income, Sara had to find a way to support herself financially. She trained as a kinesiologist, balancing her new work with being mother to her two young teenage children. But she still needed a way to pay the larger bills. With her experience of buying and restoring wrecked buildings like the Haven, it seemed clear that property development could be the way. It would fulfil her need to create and still give her time for other things. Ever the adventurer, she is now starting a property development company in Montenegro.

Keeping a proper balance in life is always Sara's goal – the Buddha in her still life is there to remind her of the essential connectedness of things. 'That's what it's all about.' The Buddha comes, she says, from Bali, her favourite island, where the people are so connected with earth and spirit that they are an example to us all. Beside her in the photograph are her three wise monkeys, her guardians as she calls them, to keep her seeing only good in the world. They shine in the light, she points out.

She is now semi-detached from her charity, while still a trustee and a source of ideas, knowing, she says confidently, that the trust and its operations are in very capable hands. She is free to move on. Some doors will surely open, once she knows where she wants to go. It is hard to resist Sara under full steam.


## Still Life

Dog painting – Bel, 'a noble dog', her gallery
The Haven – her charity
Polo ball and painting – her children's enthusiasms
Buddha – connectedness and balance
Three wise monkeys – her guardians
Camellia – many layers make a whole

# Michael de Giorgio

It was the end of the summer term in 2002. Michael de Giorgio was picking up his son from St Paul's School in west London. As he waited, he looked at the expanse of playing fields that were going to lie there unused for the next two months. His mind went back to the Easter break he had spent in Nice and the lines of empty shuttered mansions he saw there. 'What a waste,' he had thought then, and now, as he gazed at those magnificent playing fields, he was struck by the same sense of wasted assets. On the spur of the moment he asked the school if it would allow him to use its facilities for the benefit of local youths. St Paul's agreed to give him a two-week trial period.

Mike spoke to the local police and, with the help of one impressive young police constable, identified some fifty young people who lived on the estate at the back of the school and who would be at a loose end during the summer with nothing to do. He enrolled a head coach who brought in a group of assistants. Between them they laid on a two-week multi-sport programme at the school, with a friend, Justin Byam Shaw, keeping an eye on it all because, as luck would have it, the fortnight that the school had allocated were the weeks when Mike himself would be away on holiday. Another friend, who worked at *The Times*, persuaded the editor to do an article on the project. It quoted the local police as saying that crime had fallen during those two weeks. 'Of course,' says Mike, 'if you take fifty youths off the streets for whatever reason, lots of activity will stop.' Nonetheless, by the end of the programme, Mike and Justin knew they had an idea worth pursuing. Mike had paid half of the costs himself, and had persuaded the Garfield Weston Foundation to fund the other half.

Mike could do this because he had recently sold his business and was looking for something to do. Justin was in the same situation. Both were in their mid-forties with energy and unfulfilled ambitions to make a difference in some way. Now they had a project that might do just that, but to allow them to donate money to it tax-free they needed to make it a charitable activity. It happened that Justin had an unused charitable foundation called the Greenhouse Foundation, which they used until the project gained charitable status itself, but the Greenhouse name endured and has since gone from strength to strength.

'That first fortnight went well,' says Mike, 'so we started an Easter programme at St Paul's, and weekend programmes, too, which I looked after myself. It was mainly football at first and just St Paul's but by the next year we were at King's College School Wimbledon, St Paul's Girls' School, Haberdashers' Aske's, Elstree, New Cross and Oxford.' They also ran one week of drama at St Paul's and at Latymer. Justin, who ran one of the drama weeks, said that it was one of the most satisfying experiences of his life, but because it only involved twelve kids at most it was never going to be economically sensible as a major part of the project. As the programme developed to include half-terms, they began to go directly to secondary state schools rather than housing estates in order to provide a more ongoing experience for the young people.

The focus of the project had now, in its second year, moved on from utilizing the underused facilities of independent schools to offering sports and arts activities in a variety of settings to develop the life and social skills of eleven- to sixteen-year-olds, none of whom had the advantages enjoyed by the pupils of independent schools. Greenhouse aims to fill some of that gap wherever possible. Table tennis, for example, has become an important element of the programme in many state schools, one that can be played on the schools' own premises, after school hours, at weekends and in holidays. It is exciting to see the enthusiasm that table tennis can generate in schools in areas such as Tower Hamlets where independent schools do not exist and where playing fields are in short supply. Greenhouse now sees itself as a fully fledged community project for young people, operating mainly in London where there is a huge unsatisfied need for the sort of projects it is pioneering, working with youth groups as well as schools. Interestingly, observes Mike, the government has recently begun to adopt much of the Greenhouse agenda, placing a new emphasis on exercise, attacking obesity and finding activities to involve the young after formal classes have ended.

After three years the model is still evolving and Greenhouse may yet spread beyond London. The staff is growing. There are already ten full-time table tennis coaches, three full-time multi-sport coaches and some sixty part time, with three office staff. Still small, but getting bigger. The funding, too, is developing. At first it relied on personal donations from Mike and Justin, then from private foundations, but to be sustainable in the longer term it needs to develop its independent sources of finance. This may include using Greenhouse's expertise to sell its services to businesses, such as running staff sports days or team-building events. Greenhouse can also charge for some of its activities. Schools, for example, pay half of the costs of the table tennis programmes. The team is looking for corporate sponsors and is exploring the opportunity of government funding, but not, Mike insists, at the cost of its independence. You cannot live for ever, he says, by relying on people's generosity. Mike gives the project most of his time and some of his money, but this again cannot be guaranteed to last. The project must eventually pay its own way; in the meantime he is careful to grow it only as fast as he can finance it. Mike is still a practical businessman. He is also, importantly, an 'operator'. 'You have to roll up your sleeves and get involved, turn up, talk to the coaches, the children, the head teacher, the police. You have to get their input, learn from them directly. Most charities raise money to give to other organizations to use. I'm just not interested in doing that.'

The future is full of possibilities. Greenhouse could grow to include more sites, or more sports. Other organizations are eager to merge with it, but Mike is cautious of surrendering independence. He needs, however, to free himself from day-to-day involvement in order to have time to refine the model and to grow the business. The immediate need, therefore, is for a chief operating officer. Looking back, to where they started only three years before, he can see that no business plan could have foreseen where they have reached. Businesses grow organically, but they need careful husbandry and this is, as Mike well knows, a true business, albeit one with a very social purpose.

And business is what Mike de Giorgio does well, although that could not necessarily have been predicted. He was born in Malta, the fourth of five children. His father was an architect. At age ten Mike was sent to school in Britain, at Stonyhurst, a Jesuit boarding school. He feels sure that some of the Jesuit values of self-discipline, concern for the poor and disdain for materialism must have rubbed off on him during his eight years there. Then, after a year teaching in a prep school, he went to Bristol University where he studied Politics and met his future wife, Marianne, an Australian, whom he married four years later. At this point there were no signs of a yearning for business. But necessity is indeed the mother of invention. Having met Marianne, he wanted to stay in Britain but he had no work permit. The only solution was to continue his studies, but he also needed to earn money, so he considered law or accountancy. He settled on the latter and joined Price Waterhouse in order to train. It was not a happy three years. Accountancy was a means to an end, not something he wanted to do as a career. Besides, he found it gruelling, uncreative of work. Marianne complained at the time that he was no longer the person she had met at university. So he left as soon as he qualified and, with a Maltese acquaintance, set up his own business. The entrepreneurial streak in him was breaking out. 'Quite honestly, it was a business that we had no qualifications for at all. We advised Maltese, and later others, who wanted to set up business in Britain, but the great thing about doing these things when you are young is that you are free to make mistakes, you have no responsibilities or financial commitments.' It turned out, however, that the two partners had very different philosophies for the growth of their business and soon split.

Mike moved on to create his own company, Portman. 'My own name was too complicated and I was driving through Portman Square one day and thought that was a good name. I looked it up at Companies House and found it was available.' The company helped businesses and lawyers to establish in Britain by providing advice, making connections and acting as a portal to the UK. It helped that, like most Maltese, Mike spoke several European languages, albeit 'badly and often in the same sentence', as he says. That was in 1986 and over the next fifteen years the business pros-pered until at its height it was employing some fifty-five people. 'I never wanted it to get too big. I'm not a manager, more a creator.' Nor was he hungry for great wealth. 'Coming from a middle-class professional background I have always lived comfortably, but I have never hankered after the things that others feel to be important.'

In 2001 he sold the business and began to look for something to do. Greenhouse is a large part of the answer. Will he get involved in business again? 'If you want to spend money you have to earn money, and I probably will get into business again. It depends on how much you want to spend. At the moment, however, it's a lot of fun, trying to build up this business model for Greenhouse. It's different because there is no competitor, not for our type of community.'

What drives this unusual man? His still life offers some clues. At the centre is a tomato. It represents his Maltese family and the values he inherited from it. 'Every time I go back to Malta I will sleep in my old room and will still be woken up with a glass of hot milk in the morning, then my mother will cut up that tomato to cook me a traditional Maltese meal. Other than my wife, my mother has probably been the most important influence in my life. She is very religious, an extraordinary woman with the ability to get on with the high and the humble. At present she talks every day with a prostitute there, trying to keep her off the streets. My father is also very involved in charity work with the Knights of Malta but it's my mother who gets her hands dirty, who is a true operator.'

At the back of the still life is a drawing of his London home. It is his hope that this home will play as large a part in his children's lives as his Maltese home and family have in his. From families we learn our values, even if they take some time to develop. Mike is clearly a man driven by his values as much as by his ambitions.

The shoes are the sign of an active man, interested in sport. He plays football twice a week, as well as tennis and badminton, and he runs. Sport, he feels, particularly team sports, exemplified by Chelsea Football Club is crucial to our development. It provides a positive outlet for our energies, teaches the value of hard work, discipline and respect for others.

The mobile phone is the ubiquitous symbol of our time, the lifeline for an independent operator. Constant communication is a necessity in his world of networks, and Mike is good at it.

Dominating the still life is an oleander plant. The oleander grows prolifically in Malta, it is hardy and very vigorous. In Malta they talk of *grinta* or true grit, something that he feels is essential to success in life. 'I am a little worried that my children may not have it.' Mike, however, has lots of it, as well as the altruism that was sown in Malta and nurtured by the Jesuits. The combination is clearly effective.

## *Still Life*

Tomato – Malta and family values
Shoes – activity and sport
Chelsea FC – team sport, discipline and hard work
House drawing – home and family
Mobile phone – communication and networking
Oleander plant – hardy, vigorous and enduring

# Tony Falkenstein

When Tony Falkenstein visited London in 2001 on sabbatical with his family, he not only bought himself a London taxi to use back home in Auckland, New Zealand, but he also learnt about the schemes to encourage more enterprise teaching in British schools. Something clicked in his mind. He had just been reading a global survey from the London Business School that ranked New Zealand as number two in entrepreneurship in the world, if measured by start-ups, but only 40 per cent of those start-ups lasted more than four years. Kiwi dreams clearly needed to be backed up with better business skills if they were to come to fruition. New Zealand also ranked close to the bottom in management and business education with very little at school level

An entrepreneur himself, with a record of as many failures as successes, but also an experienced manager, Tony could understand the problem, but he was now in a position to do something about it. He had learnt the hard way, by experience, but he wonders what would have happened if he had had the early training that he is now hoping to give to the next generation. He is in no doubt that it would have helped. 'I was so naïve.' Three years after that London visit he successfully floated his latest company, Just Water International, on the New Zealand Stock Exchange, and was left with seventy-five per cent of the shares. He gave NZ$1 million of those shares to his old school, Onehunga High, on condition that it created a stand-alone business studies centre, teaching students in the top four forms up to diploma level.

The centre would have its own building with internet facilities to link with similar schools in the US and Israel for student chat-room sessions. Prominent local business people would address classes each week and overseas leaders could interact with students on screen. It should be self-funding after three years with fees from foreign students, who would be charged NZ$20,000 a year but would be restricted to twenty per cent of the places. Other income would come from short courses for the surrounding community.

Onehunga High was an interesting place to start. It is in a relatively poor area of Auckland and has a mix of thirty different nationalities. As Tony said, 'If you're the son of a plumber in Onehunga, you don't know anything different. We're saying, you don't have to be just a plumber in Onehunga. You can be a supplier to the world.' But it was where Tony had started out, even though, he readily admits, he didn't shine at school. He has more than made up for that now. 'What I've done in Onehunga,' he says, 'is the most satisfying thing I've ever done. The results have been phenomenal.'

It didn't stop there, however. He also went to the other end of the scale, to the high-profile business schools in the university sector. He gave the same amount of shares to the University of Auckland Business School and to the Unitec School of Management and Entrepreneurship. To back it up he recruited a number of top business people to be trustees of the money. Armed with these initiatives, he went to talk to the Ministry of Education to try to persuade the government to make business and entrepreneurship part of the national curriculum for every school. The New Zealand Education Minister plans to make this happen over the next couple of years.

If the imaginative flair of the Kiwis can be turned into continuing business success stories, some of the credit must go to the ideas that were sown in Tony Falkenstein's head that time in London. Not that he is interested in claiming any credit for himself. He was, he says, always a shy lad. He is now a modest man, just grateful for the way his life has turned out.

It has been, by any standards, an interesting life so far. Tony was the third child of German parents who emigrated to New Zealand in the 1930s. After a Commerce degree at Auckland University he set off for London to make his fortune and, he hoped, to travel. Travel he certainly did. The agency he visited on his first day in London offered him a job helping to organize the IceCapades and International Holidays on Ice in South America and at its Vienna office. Aged twenty-three, he found he had eighty of the world's top skaters under his care. He was still an innocent in the world of business. 'I used to carry an old Lufthansa bag around with me that, at times, might have had $100,000 in it, without a thought that anyone might rob me.' Luckily, they didn't, but, unluckily, he became ill. Worried about South American hospitals and the stories that they sold organs for profit, he ran back to New Zealand, found that he had only a mild attack of glandular fever and was up and about in a few days, but that was the end of that short career. Fortunate, perhaps, in the light of what came after, but he had already learnt something about managing people, even if they were ice-skating stars.

Back home in New Zealand, aged twenty-four, he got a job with Polaroid on the strength of what was now his 'international experience', first as finance manager, later as the youngest ever general manager of any of its subsidiaries. 'I liked being the boss,' he admits, adding that perhaps because of his shyness he needed an official title to allow him to show what he was capable of. After nine years there he was headhunted to run a business called Optical Holdings, which made and sold optical frames, where he found himself faced with a major turnaround operation. A conservative man, Tony thought himself bold when he bought 20,000 shares in the company at 33 cents each. For two years running they were the biggest growth stock on the New Zealand Stock Exchange. Twelve years later they were worth NZ$12 and he bailed out with NZ$600,000 profit in his pocket. It was time to start his entrepreneurial career. He was in his mid-thirties and recently married.

He formed his own company and went looking for products. Attracted first by the new Swatch brand of watches, he tried to get the agency for New Zealand but discovered it had already gone to someone else. Nothing daunted, he went to Hong Kong and found a distributor there for a competitor brand, Zee, which made red-faced watches with a Z slashed across them, and decided to take on Swatch with Zee in New Zealand. During his time with Optical Holdings he had made good contacts with the pharmacies and they happily sold his watches by the thousand after a high-profile advertising campaign. In one month he sold 27,000 compared with Swatch's 6000. 'I had NZ$1 million in my pocket by Christmas,' he remembers.

Then disaster. The straps started to fall off and the watches stopped working. The Hong Kong distributor had disappeared, leaving Tony to honour a two-year guarantee on every watch. All his money, and more, was used up. 'It really was the low point of my life,' he says, redeemed only by the birth of a daughter to him and his wife, Heather. It might be safer to be a salaried manager instead, he reckoned, and for three years he ran a health-food business in Australia, before returning to New Zealand to do some major surgery on a trading company, until the stock market and the company crashed on the fateful Black Monday in October 1987, leaving him with no option but to start his own business again.

A week after the stock market crash, with one salesperson and a secretary, he started renting fax machines to offices. He would buy the machines for NZ$2,000 and rent them over two years for a total of NZ$4,000. Business boomed at first, but then companies started to buy their own machines, prices fell and Tony saw the writing on the wall. He would have to find another product that he could rent to companies. He chose water – bottles, coolers and filters for offices – and started Just Water. At that time, the early 1990s, only 25 per cent of offices in New Zealand had water coolers, although they had been a regular feature of office life in the US for years. Tony was ahead of the curve. Just Water removes the chlorine through a carbon filter, then puts the water in small bottles or in large containers and delivers it to offices.

This time it worked. The business grew steadily. In 2004 the company bought Aqua Cool, New Zealand's largest bottled water delivery company, the prelude to going public later that year. Tony is now content to leave running the company to others who are, he believes, better able to manage a going concern. 'I haven't got many talents but I do have the ideas,' he says, so he brought in an outside chairman and appointed competent managers, leaving himself free to move on to other things, including his own particular brand of philanthropy. 'In your business life,' he believes, 'you have to create your own little revolution every five years or else you stand still.' He is already on to his next idea, expanding into Australia and then internationally – if he has enough time left over from reforming the educational priorities of New Zealand's schools.

He used to wonder whether he might have been better off staying as a corporate employee, but he has always been an entrepreneur at heart, and, he says, an eccentric and a bit of an exhibitionist – hence the taxi, an exotic vehicle on the streets of Auckland. 'I never really grew up,' he says, 'I've always been a daydreamer. And I really loved my time in the ice-show business.' Besides, entrepreneurship was in the family. His mother was dynamic, very outgoing and the entrepreneur of the two parents, starting her own little businesses.

But life, he says, has to be about more than work. 'Nothing too extreme' might be his motto for a good life. Read the papers, take an interest in the world outside, don't get too mesmerized by your own affairs, keep fit, eat sensibly and take up gardening. Gardening, he reflects, carries its own messages for an entrepreneur. 'If you muck up one season, you just start again.'

Perhaps, however, the best clue to this enterprising man is the tea that features in his still life. 'I bring tea to my wife in bed every morning. That is in part the celebration of a happy marriage but it is also because I'm a giver. I believe that what you give always comes back in some way. I give shares in the business to all my employees.' And, he might add, he gives generously of his time and money to boost the future of young New Zealanders. He has a neat phrase – 'I'm better at being a Go-giver than a Go-getter.'

Most people would say that he is good at both. As for the future, it could be summed up as Today New Zealand, Tomorrow the World, something that might be as true of his country's youth as it will, he hopes, be of his business.

## Still Life

Model taxi – the London trip, eccentricity and the showman
Newspaper – well informed and interested
Muesli – healthy living
Tennis ball – sport and a balanced life
Tea – happy marriage and pleasure in giving
Rose – beauty, gardening and the experimental life

# Jeff Gambin

Jeff Gambin loves food – and people. Once he fed rich people at his fashionable Sydney restaurants. Now he cooks for the poor. In 1993 he spent Christmas giving dinner to thirty homeless people from the back of his car. He bought gifts for each person and put a 'few bucks in an envelope'.

Fast-forward 12 years and he was expecting to feed 1,500 people at the annual Just Enough Faith Christmas party. It is at Christmas that Jeff and his wife Alina's commitment to providing hot and cold gourmet meals to 400 of Sydney's homeless and helpless becomes even more important, with 80 per cent of the project funded from his own resources.

It had been a long journey from Assam in Northern India where Jeff grew up. He is, he says proudly, the son of Tibetan parents who were tea planters; his father was a Gurkha, stern and not too inclined to give praise, his mother just the opposite, warm and loving. They lived well, he remembers, with some fifteen servants, whose children were his friends. He hunted with a bow and arrow and kept a couple of lynx cubs as pets. It was, he says, an idyllic childhood in which he was allowed to try his hand at anything. The adventurous spirit that grew in him then has never died. At the numerous boarding schools he attended he was a rebel, better at sport than exams, until the day came when the head of yet another new school challenged him on his arrival. 'We know your reputation as a rebel,' he said, 'but now I would like you to be captain of your new house. Do you think you are up to it?' 'That man changed my life,' Jeff recalls. The rebel turned into a leader and his house won the house championship. From then on he became a high achiever, representing India as a schoolboy in a number of sports.

From India he went to university at Cambridge where, unplanned, he qualified as a chef and a pilot as well as an entomologist. His dictatorial father had insisted that he study either medicine or engineering, so Jeff, rebelling again, chose entomology, only to find that his father had cut off his allowance. Nothing daunted Jeff found work in the kitchens of London's Dorchester hotel at night, juggling studies at Cambridge, work at the Dorchester and flying lessons. It took him five years to finish a four-year course but he did it, earning himself the nickname of the 'buggered up flying chef' (bugs as in entomology) and leaving him with his life-long passions of cooking and flying.

'Don't come back to India,' his father said. 'There is nothing for you here. There are only two countries, Canada or Australia.' 'Why those two?' asked Jeff. 'Because I fought with them in the war.' It was as good a reason as any. Jeff chose Australia, loved the friendly people and the sunny skies and never looked back. But the adventurer in him was still alive.

When he first arrived in Australia he started work flying as a crop-duster, and flying remained his passion even when it later became a hobby rather than a livelihood. He was a dare-devil pilot who, one day, decided to fly under Sydney Harbour Bridge. As he levelled out at about seventy-five feet and was about to start his run through the bridge he saw to his dismay that there were flotillas of little boats underneath him. It was a regatta. Then he knew he was in trouble, but by then it was too late to stop. Flying through the bridge was illegal, he knew, but he had not intended it to be so public. When he landed he was met by an array of officials. He was given a hefty fine and had his licence revoked. 'I felt as if my legs had been cut off,' he says, 'because flying had been my life.'

'I sat there with my scotch and wondered how I could turn this to my advantage. I decided to use the time when I would not be flying to pay more attention to my restaurants, to raise the bar.' For by then Jeff had indulged in his other passion, food. While still crop-dusting he had opened a roadhouse café in Western Australia and then a restaurant in Perth, the St George. He moved to Adelaide, opened another restaurant, leased a few thousand acres, fattened his own cattle and got married, had children and bought three houses. He was successful and life was good. Then it was Sydney, a hotel and yet more restaurants, including a memorable one called the Chelsea.

He was irrepressible – on a visit to Cairns he could not find an Indian restaurant, so he started one, for 700 people, with a gala opening featuring Rock Hudson and Lee Marvin, who were in town at the time. Only the day before he discovered that no one had ordered enough plates. Cairns did not have that many plates, even if he borrowed them from all the other restaurants. So Jeff got banana leaves from a nearby plantation and served the food on these – to great acclaim. As he himself says, he has always had that extra spark of energy and imagination, though it didn't always turn out so well.

Aged forty-five, he was at the top of the pile, with his restaurants, seventeen thoroughbred racehorses ('I have always loved horses and the sport of kings') and a golden Rolls-Royce Corniche. Then it happened. One cold night in July he went down to the park to sit on a bench and think out a business dilemma. A homeless man, mistaking Jeff for another homeless person, offered him his blanket. 'What about you?' Jeff protested. 'I'm used to the cold,' he replied, 'you aren't.' Then he walked away. That man had given Jeff his only possession without even knowing his name. Somehow his business problems seemed insignificant. The next night Jeff went back to the park, met his new friend again. They talked.

Jeff spent the next few weeks living rough himself on occasional nights to experience this unfamiliar side of life. He came back resolved to sell all his restaurants, racehorses and car and to start cooking for the homeless instead. It took some time to complete the deals but from that day on Jeff has never missed a day, feeding the hungry people on the streets of Sydney. Not long after that epochal park bench meeting Jeff met Alina, now his wife, who had heard him being interviewed on the radio. 'I thought to myself,' she says, 'that it was about time I got up and did something useful myself. One thing led to another. I ended up meeting Jeff, just to see what I could do as far as helping the homeless went. And here I am, in full-time occupation. See where things lead. I keep reminding him, all I ever wanted to do was to help the homeless people and I got you in the bargain. Oh, it's amazing.' And the best man at their wedding was the man who gave Jeff his blanket.

Over time Jeff and Alina created their own charity, Just Enough Faith Foundation (JEFF), to undertake the work. In spite of its name, the charity is not affiliated to any religious organization, nor does it receive any government funding. Today, with the help of a sous-chef, a kitchen hand and several volunteers they prepare 400 meals every night. There's a different choice of nine dishes every night – all of excellent quality, something the foody in Jeff insists upon, and offering a balanced diet. Twice a week, Jeff does the cooking himself, to maintain the standards but also because that is still his passion. 'In fact,' he says, 'I've never enjoyed cooking as much as I do now.' Two vans take the food to the corner of St Mary's Road and the Yurong Parkway where the hungry and homeless are waiting. 'When I drive up and see these people,' says Jeff, 'lining up and waiting for a meal, that has never ceased to sadden me. Because can you imagine the humiliation they must be going through? I mean, just to line up for a bowl of food. But when I get out of the van I feel happy because thank God I am here and I am able to give them the food and the time, a cigarette, listen to them, chat to them – companionship.'

'People sometimes say to us,' Alina comments, 'why do you do it every night? Then Jeff says, "I like to eat every day, how about you?" That's a fact, that's a reality.'

Jeff and Alina pay for most of the food out of their own pockets with some help in kind from the food suppliers. It costs them Aus$15,000 a week. They also run a 25-acre farm outside Sydney left to them by a nun in her will, who wanted it to be used for a charitable purpose. It is staffed by some volunteers and a few of the homeless. The idea is for the farm to be self-sufficient with vegetables and livestock and to be a place for the homeless to get back some dignity and learn some life-skills along the way. That is because their overall objective, as Jeff explains, is much more than just feeding the homeless. 'If we just went out and there and fed them and did nothing else, that would be like throwing chips to seagulls.' It's about giving them hope, about helping them regain respect by giving them counselling, housing and training. Recently, Jeff created a computer training facility at the Rozelle Centre where the kitchens are now located, so that he could give some of the homeless people the skills that would offer them a new start in life. Jeff and Alina spend a lot of their time now scanning newspapers for job advertisements, assisting people to prepare for interviews and speaking to prospective employers on their behalf.

In the twelve years since he started this work Jeff calculates that Just Enough Faith has taken more than 1,200 individuals off the streets and helped them find meaningful work and permanent housing. But there are thought to be over 100,000 people in Australia without a regular place to stay, for a range of reasons that defy some of the easy stereotypes. Over 20 per cent choose to be homeless, 45 per cent are mentally ill, but the remaining 35 per cent are just poor and destitute. Jeff will often meet professional people lining up at his vans, people who have lost their homes and families through redundancy, gambling or alcoholism. There is still a lot of work to be done.

More money is needed, for better equipment and more produce, and Jeff and Alina are, for the first time, actively seeking corporate financial assistance. But Jeff, ever the entrepreneur, has also started a new venture called Just Enough Ink to supply printer ink to big firms. The idea is that the profits will all go to the charity and will supplement his personal money as funding for the project when he and Alina grow older. He has already signed up a number of large corporate customers. It will be a fine example of business as philanthropy.

Jeff has received a number of awards for his work, including being celebrated as the Unsung Hero amid Sydney's millennium celebrations on New Year's Eve 1999 and as Humanitarian of the Year in 2000, but he was particularly touched when, in 2000, the year of the Sydney Olympics, the Mayor of Sydney asked him to carry the Olympic torch through the city streets. That night he excused himself from the celebration ball in order to take the torch down to his van to show it to his homeless friends. Forget the celebrities, these were the people who mattered most to him.

## Still Life

The Olympic torch – recognition and celebration
Horse book – love of horses and racing
Tray of spices – passion for food and cooking
Whisky bottle – relaxation and his father's drink
Watch – time is precious
Frangipani flowers - childhood in India

# Ram Gidoomal

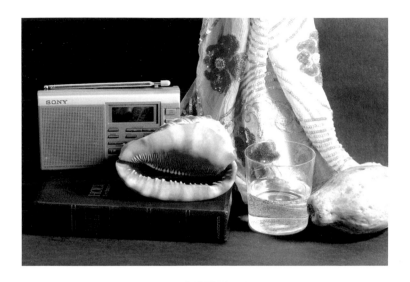

In 1987 Ram Gidoomal flew to Mumbai to buy prawns for his business. He was 37 years old and running a family business in Scotland employing 600 people there and 7,000 worldwide. In ten years he had helped build it from a turnover of a few million pounds to over £100 million, trading in commodities with the developing world, with interests that included vineyards in France and tea estates in India. He had come a long way from the sixteen-year-old refugee from Kenya whose family of fifteen had just been forced to leave a comfortable life in that country to live in four rooms above a newsagent's in Shepherd's Bush. His family were 'twice immigrants'. They had had to leave India at the time of partition, where they had lived in a palace in Hyderabad Sind, and moved first to Pakistan and then on to Kenya, where they had prospered and where Ram was born. They had now been forced to come to Britain where they had to start all over again.

On the last day of his visit to Mumbai Ram met a group of

Christian pastors who took him around the city's shanty town, its slums and ghettos. He saw child prostitutes sitting in cages, locked in by their pimps and on display. He saw little kids living in cardboard boxes and some, with no way to rent even a box, sleeping on the pavement – if they could find a space. 'I was absolutely devastated by the appalling sights I saw. How come that at the age of thirty-seven, although I was an international businessman who had been to university, I could be so unaware of the hardship that over a billion people suffer?' Ram recalls.

During the first-class plane journey back, he couldn't face the caviar and champagne on offer. He said to himself, 'How could I be a Christian in such conspicuous luxury, doing nothing about what I have seen? Could I coexist on the planet allowing a group of human beings to live in the way I have just witnessed, while doing nothing about it?' Ram recalls, 'I was faced with a choice of personal futures, and I knew what I had to do.'

Back home he talked to his wife, Sunita. They reflected that they could not spend even the interest that they earned on their current wealth. They didn't need so much. He handed in his notice to the family business and sold his shares. 'I wanted to come out completely, although it did take five years to extract myself fully. I wanted to focus full time on social entrepreneurship. Young people were my focus, because of what I had seen in Mumbai. Seeing is believing. I was determined to see if I could offer opportunities to young people so that they could become aware, at a young age, of how privileged they were, that they could do something, of how empowered they were, and of their responsibility to those who had less.'

So he started Christmas Cracker. He and Steve Chalke – another Christian who had once visited the same slums – came up with the 'Eat Less – Pay More' idea, a temporary restaurant where customers were invited to pay more for less food, first world prices for third-world grub, with all the proceeds going to famine relief in the developing world. Being a businessman, Ram immediately thought 'franchise'. If hamburger restaurants could be nationwide, why not charity restaurants? In 1989 Christmas Cracker was able to mobilize over 20,000 young British people to create more than 100 temporary 'Cracketerias', raising £400,000 to help the poor of India.

In the following years they increased the number of restaurants to 400, and set up nearly 100 community radio stations, 'Tune In – Pay Out' Radio Cracker, to spread the message to surrounding homes and draw people to the 'Eat Less – Pay More' Crackerterias. The radio stations operated under special restricted service licences from the Radio Authority. If you wanted a record played, you pledged money. If you wanted to sponsor a programme, you could. A young person would go around on a bike collecting requests and cheques and bring them back to the station. A young engineer at London's Imperial College made the transmitters, for which Gidoomal raised the money and passed them on to the stations.

But, says Ram, the real purpose was not just fundraising. He wanted to excite young people, to make them aware of the issues faced by those in the poorer parts of the world, and to give them the experience of social entrepreneurship at an early age so that it would become embedded in them, something that they would never forget. 'And we wanted the kids to be creative and innovative, to see that as a key part of social entrepreneurship.' Even simple things like writing a cheque or opening a bank account were new experiences for some of the young people involved. The project entailed a week of business training and a week of theological reflection on the question of poverty and the response to it, led by local church groups. It was meant to be a one-off one-year project but it continued for seven years, mobilizing over 50,000 teenagers to raise over £5 million for the developing world. It was supported by £2 million worth of help and grants to cover the costs of the project from business and community groups.

The *Financial Times* quoted him that first year as saying, 'The creative use of business skills and links makes things happen. It gives me all the excitement of deal-making, not to make money for myself now, but to get other people excited, getting them to go beyond themselves.' Ram Gidoomal is an instinctive businessman. He sees opportunities where others see problems. 'For me the glass is always half-full.' He is also, and importantly, a committed Christian who lives his beliefs and is impelled to offer his skills and his time to those less fortunate than himself. It is also part of his philosophy to involve as many others in his causes, so that they become stakeholders and share in what he sees as the privilege of helping others. In that way he is, he hopes, sowing the seeds for a better future.

From restaurants and radio stations he moved on to other imaginative ideas. The Really Useful Present Stores sold Fairtrade products in high streets over Christmas. Then, one year he organized an Alternative Christmas in June, to help with projects specifically in Africa. The idea was to give each participating group of children £1, donated by HSBC bank, with the challenge to see how much they could generate from that meagre investment in forty-eight hours, starting on a Friday evening. Over 400 groups took part, and when they all reported back they had turned just over £400 into £125,000, by washing cars, selling sandwiches, canvassing neighbours for donations – to Ram, a living example of the biblical parable of the talents. The idea was to set stretching challenges for young people for noble purposes. 'They always delivered,' he says.

His neat way of branding his projects caught on. Christian Aid, for example, launched 'Wash for Dosh', where church groups set up car-washing schemes. To help the victims of an earthquake in Maharashtra, Ram arranged with GMTV's Breakfast Television a one week programme headed by their fitness instructor, Mr Motivator, and using the strapline 'Lose Pounds, Give Pounds'. People around the country were urged to sign up with their local fitness club to give as much as they lost in weight in the week. In that week they raised half a million pounds. The funds were used to build a hospital in Maharashtra and GMTV went out to film its construction. The *Daily Mirror* also got involved, asking for volunteers to go out to help, creating more stakeholder involvement in what is now the Prya GMTV Hospital – Prya being the young girl who survived three days in the earthquake rubble before being rescued alive.

Ram's aim had always been to raise awareness of troublesome issues, and he now set out to reach a wider audience, firstly by writing – his book *Sari 'n' Chips* explored the challenges and dilemmas facing Asian immigrants, drawing on his own experience as a Kenyan Asian – and secondly through politics. He became the leader of the Christian Peoples Alliance and ran for Mayor in the London elections. His aim, for he never realistically expected to be elected, was to reach out to groups who were disconnected from the political process. He put forward policies that emphasized compassion, reconciliation, social justice, empowerment and respect for life. He ran twice and won a very respectable 100,000 votes on both occasions.

In the meantime he was becoming increasingly concerned by the plight of refugees. One third of refugees with the right to work have degrees, he points out, one third are qualified professionals, who could add a lot to society, yet the unemployment in this group averages 26 per cent (six times the national average) because of the stigma that they carry in the eyes of employers. 'They are the lepers of the tewnty-first century,' he claims. His entrepreneurial instincts came into play again. He helped set up a charity called the Employability Forum, which brings together senior figures in business, government, trades unions and local councils to seek practical solutions to the issues that affect refugees and asylum seekers.

Then there was the Boost Bond, another initiative in which he got involved, which sets out to help people in inner cities and deprived communities into jobs and homes. Interest-free money is raised from individuals and local businesses, with guarantees to pay back the money in full after five years, and with permission to use the anticipated interest to develop small businesses and offer mentoring help and other practical support. Gidoomal was impressed by the first Bond Scheme pioneered in Sheffield and agreed to chair a fund to help residents in the London boroughs of Tower Hamlets, Hackney and Newham. He brought leading business figures around the table to raise the necessary support and resources. Chancellor of the Exchequer Gordon Brown offered 11 Downing Street to launch the scheme. Merchant bank Nomura was present at the launch and was so impressed that it offered £1 million on the spot. There was no government money involved. The event raised £2 million, guaranteed by the Royal Bank of Canada, and the money was then loaned out at business rates to organizations like the Places for People Group, which builds affordable housing and provides incubator units for local entrepreneurs. Ram's own experience in the family business has made him aware of the importance of mentoring. 'It was part and parcel of our upbringing. It is one reason why East Indian Asians have been so successful over here. Added to which, we Sindhis are all entrepreneurs by nature.'

His Sindhi heritage is obviously important to him, as is his partnership with Sunita. It was her family that provided him with his early business opportunities and she is an active and important partner in all his philanthropic ventures. 'I need to listen to her.' His father died when he was very young, so he was brought up by an uncle who gave him a lot of early responsibility. He learnt early on that he could make a difference and soon found himself, at that time a Hindu, the head boy of a Muslim school. Making a difference was to become a habit, first in business and then, after Mumbai, in the voluntary sector. He was never to forget that much of the world has insufficient food, too few seeds of hope and a lack of leadership. He has spent his life since then doing something about that.

Nowadays he remains involved in the business world, as director of a number of companies, but gives at least two-thirds of his time to his philanthropic ventures. 'I like to be in touch with the latest business ideas, which I can then apply to the voluntary sector. But my energy comes from Sunita, from the Bible and the example of servant leadership that Jesus gave us, and from my gratitude that my life has been so fortunate.'

## Still Life

A Bible – his Christian driving force
Sunita's wedding sari – Sunita, love and giving
Glass of water – optimism and opportunity
Short-wave radio – links with the world
Seashell – Mombasa and family heritage
Papaya – food and seeds of the future

# Carolyn Hayman

C arolyn Hayman had what she calls her light-bulb moment in
2002. She was sitting on a grant-making committee that had
just agreed eight grants to peace organizations, all of them in London.
Why, she wondered, were they all in London? Was there not some
way of getting the money to the organizations and individuals in
the countries where the conflicts were actually taking place, skip-
ping over the bodies in the middle – disintermediation as it is called
in the business world that she came from? So, like the entrepreneur
that she is, she went out looking for someone with the same idea
and she found Scilla Elworthy. Scilla was a social entrepreneur who
had founded the Oxford Research Group in the 1980s to investigate the murky world of nuclear weapons policy and would later,
in 2003, be awarded the Niwano Peace Prize in Tokyo for her work
on non-violent approaches to conflict. In 2001 she was already
pursuing the idea that was to become Peace Direct, which was
launched at the Royal Opera House on 11 September 2002.

'Scilla and I are very different,' Carolyn says, 'she is more interested in the individuals whereas I am more analytical. It could have been very difficult but there is now a lot of mutual respect, and we work very well together.' Carolyn, Scilla and a number of other people worked to build Peace Direct, initially helped by £100,000 of Carolyn's money, to be paid out over three years, and then by a similar contribution from Scilla's Niwano Trust money. Once the organization was established, with a board of trustees, Carolyn applied for the job of chief executive and was formally appointed, while Scilla remains as a very active trustee. Peace Direct is now Carolyn's full-time day job, as she backs up her philanthropy with her time and skills.

Carolyn has come full circle in her life, back to the beginnings of her career in what was then the Ministry of Overseas Development, but perhaps even further back, to her love of geography and to the wanderlust inherited from her mother who had had too little chance to indulge it. She has returned to her desire to be more than a cog in someone else's machine, to be able to make a difference to people, to her Quaker background and her wish for peace and wholeness.

Peace Direct is still small with only seven staff, eight board members and five patrons, as well as rather more eager volunteers than it can really handle, but it provides an important complement to the work of some fifty organizations in Britain alone that work on conflict resolution in some way. It focuses not on the policymakers but on those in the front line, believing that the contribution of local people committed to non-violence is crucial, but that such groups are often unnoticed, under-resourced and unsupported. In its short life Peace Direct has already funded projects in Iraq, Kenya, Indonesia, Sri Lanka and the Congo. Peace Direct can say to those who give it donations that their money will go directly to the people involved in the conflicts. They will get news of the individuals and pictures so that they can see how their money is being used.

Peace Direct also wants to raise the profile of peacebuilding. To this end it edited and published a book in 2004. *Unarmed Heroes* is a moving collection of sixteen personal testimonies by individuals who have been involved in the peaceful resolution of conflict. They include people like Jo Berry, whose father was killed by the IRA in the Brighton bombing in 1984. Jo bravely decided to meet with

Patrick Magee who planted the bomb. As a result of the personal transformation that started with this meeting Patrick Magee set up and now runs Causeway, with the help of Jo, an organization that facilitates meetings between the victims and perpetrators of violence in the Northern Ireland conflict. The hope of the book is that by telling the stories of such people more of us may see how we ourselves can make a difference. It is this desire to make a personal difference that drives Carolyn and her philanthropy, the sense, as she puts it, 'that this would not have existed except for me'.

In addition to direct support for those in the field, Peace Direct links people together. It has, for instance, linked a group in Oxfordshire with a group in Northern Uganda, to lobby to change UK policies on Uganda. It has brought the headmaster and two children from a school in Lucknow that played a major role in calming the interfaith riots in that Indian city in 1992 to share their experiences and the lessons they learnt with the citizens of Bradford and Slough, where communal tensions have been high.

Meanwhile, Scilla has been looking at what happened in Fallujah in Iraq to see what lessons can be learnt for the training of the military in future situations of that type, as well as collaborating on a play for London's Royal Court Theatre, *Talking to Terrorists*. It may be all rather simple and small-scale stuff, Carolyn says, but if they do it right they get the leverage they need to demonstrate to governments how important this sort of work can be. 'That's why,' she says, 'we have to be quite tough, to make sure that the people and groups we support are going to be good examples. It's hard, but you can't support just everyone.' It is all by way of 'getting peace out of the gutter', as she puts it, by publicizing the work of their unarmed heroes. They paid travel costs to Jonathan Holmes, for example, to go to Kenya and Uganda to shoot interviews for a film called *Perpetual Peace* to be shown back in Britain.

Was this what she always wanted to do? 'No, absolutely not. Because I'm a Quaker I have always been interested in peace, but I never thought that it would occupy the last period of my working life. I knew I wanted to do something else, and I knew I wanted to do something international because that was where I started – at the Ministry of Overseas Development.'

But that was not what she had originally intended either. In her early youth she had wanted to be a novelist, or maybe a musician, for her father, as well as being a distinguished mathematician, was descended from Felix Mendelssohn, and every member of the family was expected to play an instrument in the family quintet. Carolyn was allocated the viola, which she went on to play in the London Schools Symphony Orchestra and at Cambridge University, where she studied Classics and Philosophy. Looking back, she now understands her love of the classics with their rounded view of life and the irritation she felt with philosophy. 'Philosophers sought to interpret the world but the important thing is to change it,' she says.

The beginnings of her entrepreneurial instinct were already there, another inheritance, perhaps, from her mother, who started the Mathematics Olympics and who once took the Ministry of Defence to court. She still keeps the busts of her Mendelssohn ancestors on her mantelpiece as a reminder of her heritage and of the importance of the family, while music remains a key part of her life. She sings in a major London choir and in 2005, most poignantly given her day job, sang in a performance of Benjamin Britten's *War Requiem*.

From would-be novelist to entrepreneurial philanthropist via the civil service and a government think tank, followed by consultancy, venture capitalism and a charity for disadvantaged youth – this might seem a tortuous career line, but the path of life is often decided by random events and through all the changes in Carolyn's career there has been a constant thread of the determined initiative that defines the entrepreneur. While at Cambridge she happened to pick up a prospectus for the Institute of Development Studies that was lying around her college library and decided that that was the most interesting area to study. But before she started she wanted to go to Ethiopia with a friend, whose father rang Carolyn's father to warn him of what a dangerous place Ethiopia was. He suggested that they make their daughters abandon the trip. 'And my father said, and it was one of the nicest things I heard him say, "Well, I don't know how you think I am going to stop her."' That was, you might say, his permission for her to live an adventurous life. So off they went and it was exciting and wonderful, and the seeds of her future life were sown.

After an MSc at SOAS she joined the Ministry of Overseas Development where she soon discovered that she was not a big organization person. She read in a newspaper that the CPRS, a government think tank, was doing work on unemployment, a topic that had interested her during her degree. 'So I wrote to Kenneth Berrill (the head of the CPRS), saying, "I am truly wonderful and I'm sure you would like to employ me", which was not, apparently, what most people did, and I was lucky and got taken on.' But instead of working on unemployment she was assigned to working on the implications of the microchip and was sent around the country lecturing people on the positive benefits of this new technology. That was the springboard for her next career, which turned out to be consulting on the impact of the new technology as joint managing director of Korda and Co. with Alexander Korda, eventually sharing the running of their seed capital fund, investing in new technological ideas that might take off as businesses. 'We raised £5 million for the fund and have returned £28 million to the investors, including ourselves,' she says with quiet satisfaction. 'We financed six businesses and I found myself acting as chairman of two of them,' one of which was Cambridge Animation Systems, which made animation software and of which she was particularly fond, even though it never made any money.

She tried to raise another fund, but was unsuccessful. And at that time, 1996, none of their six companies was making any money. The excitement of venture capitalism was waning. It was time to move on to something different. Her children were away from home that weekend, so with time on her hands for once, she found herself doing something she never normally did – reading the job ads. She answered one for the chief executive of the Foyer Federation and, of course, got the job. It was another random event that shifted her life. The Foyer Federation is the umbrella body for Foyers in the UK, which provide accommodation and/or training to around 10,000 disadvantaged young people each year, as well as to the wider community. 'It was a wonderful job for me. I had been involved in homelessness. I had been involved in the first ever Open Christmases in London, setting up temporary hostels, and I had organized the Soup Kitchen. And the other side of it was education, something that I had always been interested in. So I had some credentials, even though there were those who were suspicious of the outsider.'

It was in 2000 that one of Korda's six venture companies, a German biotech business, struck lucky and made her a wealthy woman by the time the company had gone public and she had been able to sell her shares. She put most of it into her parents' small family trust from which she and her sisters dispense grants of around £40,000 a year. It is another way in which she can make a difference by investing in people, something she has always done, whether by creating jobs as a venture capitalist, or as head of the Foyer Federation and now with Peace Direct.


## Still Life

Mendelssohn busts − her heritage and family
Cake − love, affection and togetherness, and office lunches
Cycle helmet − her ride to work and place for ideas
Cartoon − Cambridge Animation, her favourite company
*War Requiem* − music and peace
Lily of the valley − her mother's flower, symbol of her care for her family

# Tom Hunter

'At thirty-seven years old I had basically achieved my life's ambitions. I had sold my business, something I had never planned to do. I had got a cheque for £260 million. My life had to start all over again. I had to re-educate myself.' Eight years later Tom Hunter is now Sir Tom Hunter, knighted in recognition of his philanthropic work. He has recently committed £53 million to the Clinton-Hunter Development Initiative for the relief of poverty in Africa, in addition to the millions he has committed to his Hunter Foundation and to its work in education in Scotland.

'This philanthropy business,' he says, 'has given a whole new meaning and purpose to wealth creation.' There is now a point, as he sees it, to making more money, if you can use it to benefit people beyond yourself. 'My wife and I have agreed that once we have seen that our children are secure, the great bulk of any money we make will go into the foundation.' And he is still making money. In 2001 he founded West Coast Capital, an investment firm with extensive holdings in retail and property companies. He is today thought to be Scotland's second-richest man.

He had come a long way in a short time from his early days behind the counter in his father's grocery store in a small mining village in Ayrshire. Everyone in the village worked in the coal mines. During the miners' strike in the 1980s there was suddenly no money and no customers. His father had to shut the shop and take to selling shoes on a market stall. Tom went off to university where he found that his studies had no relevance to the world outside. 'But the social life was great,' he adds. He tried to get a job when he left, only to discover that he seemed to be unemployable. He had, however, noticed that training shoes were an important part of his father's sales and sensed that there must be a business opportunity there.

'But I couldn't afford a shop. So I came up with the idea of selling the shoes through other people's stores. I didn't know this at the time, but such concessions, as they were called, were a well-established part of the retail world.' His girlfriend typed up a letterhead and he wrote off to a number of stores describing himself as a well-established retailer who would like to rent a space in their store. One of them asked Tom to come and see them. They liked the idea. 'I came home and said to my dad, "There's good news and there's bad news. The good news is that they want me. The bad news is that I have no money and no idea how to do this."' His father lent him £5,000, which was matched by a bank, and he used it to buy a van and some stock, which he stored in his dad's garage. That was 1984 and, luckily for Tom, trainers were about to take off as a fashion item.

His 'defining moment', as he calls it, came when that first store sat on all the money it had taken for his shoes, causing Tom a cash-flow crisis. The chairman then called him to his office. 'Tom,' he said, 'why don't we change the way we do business? Instead of us taking the money and paying you later, why don't you take the money up front and pay us commission on the sales?' At that point he was owed about £36,000. 'I agreed but never paid over any commission until the £36,000 was paid off. Six weeks later the firm went bust, by which time I was owed £148. Had it not been for that chairman's action, Tom would have been out of business almost before he had got going. On such things are our futures often decided. 'It taught me,' Tom says, 'that I would rather be lucky than clever!' Since then he has never given credit in any of his businesses.

Tom had avoided bankruptcy but had no customers. He had to get moving. Over the next five years he built up some sixty concessions with bigger stores and bigger companies all over Britain. In 1989 he opened his first store, in Paisley, on a 25-year lease, which he had to take out in his own name – massive commitment for the fledgling businessman. He soon branched out into sports clothing, which was now fashionable leisurewear, and named his stores Sports Division. After a visit to America he opened his first out-of-town large-scale sports store. By 1995 the company, with its mix of high-street shops and out-of-town stores, was turning over £36 million and making a profit of about £4 million.

The company was now the seventh biggest in the sports industry in the UK, but Tom, both then and now, thinks big. He and his team wanted to be number one. Tom approached the then number one company, Olympus Sport, and offered to buy it, but its board treated him with contempt, as beneath its notice. 'So I went to my good friend Philip Green (by then a very successful businessman) and asked him to see what he could do.' Philip negotiated a deal, bringing Tom into the room at the very last moment. 'Who's this?' the directors asked when he came in on the last day. 'He's the man with the cheque,' Philip said, 'you had better let him in.' It was a huge step. The Bank of Scotland lent him the £20 million he needed but he had to put up his company, his house, everything he had, as security. 'I was swapping a comfortable life, no borrowings, no partners, a well-established market position, for something seven times bigger, a lot of debt and losing £14 million a year.'

Three years later, by 1998, having restructured the business and turned it around, his expanded company was employing 7,500 people and turning over £350 million with a profit of about £45 million. That was when the telephone rang. Would he like to sell it? 'I had never considered selling. We were number one. But the minute I put down the phone I knew I would sell it. I don't know why, but I did.' The new owners moved the business from Scotland and a lot of jobs were lost. Tom took plenty of criticism, particularly from the press. 'That weighed heavily upon me, even

still in the land of his birth. The thistle and the cross of St Andrew are central. His pocket watch too a gift from his father, symbolizes the key part his family play in his life.

The cornerstones of his working life, however, are summed up by the other three items. The training shoes were the foundation of his wealth, the means of his philanthropy, while fellow Scot Andrew Carnegie and his *Gospel of Wealth* are his mentor and guide. Lastly, inevitably perhaps in this age, there is his mobile phone – 'It's just the way work is done,' he says.

At heart, it seems, Tom Hunter is a simple man with big dreams. He is practical and rooted in common sense, but driven by a need to do everything he can to help people to be more capable, more in control of their destiny, more able to sustain themselves and their families in an uncertain world. By instinct and background a businessman, and a very successful one, he clearly believes that wealth creation is best justified when it is used for purposes beyond the individual. He is still young. Who knows where his dreams will yet lead him?

## Still Life

Andrew Carnegie's life – a model of philanthropy
Training shoes – the foundation of his wealth
Mobile phone – how work is done
Pocket watch – family
St Andrew's cross – Scotland
Thistle – Scottish national emblem

# Mohamed Ibrahim

In March 2005 the Mobile Telecommunications Company KSC of Kuwait announced that it had reached a binding agreement to buy all the shares of Celtel International BV for $3.36 billion. Celtel was just 7 years old but was already running the largest mobile phone network in sub-Saharan Africa with operations spread over 14 countries, and 8.5 million customers at the last count. The board and management of Celtel would remain largely unchanged under the new ownership. Mo Ibrahim, the chairman and creator of the company, who owned 21.7 per cent of the shares, was going to be a wealthy man.

He immediately began to find ways to feed some of this wealth back into Africa. To do this he has set up a twin-armed family foundation. One arm will be an investment fund, investing in new African businesses, with any projects feeding back into the fund to be recycled. The best help he can give to Africa, he believes, will be the opportunity to grow businesses and create jobs. 'That is what changes people's lives in the longer term, it gives them freedom and dignity.' Indeed, that is what he has already done with Celtel, which operates in 14 African countries and employs 5,000 people with 120,000 small shopkeepers selling its prepaid vouchers.

The other arm of his foundation aims to provide practical help to projects that are too small for the big donors and too big for local charities. A $10 million state-of-the-art breast cancer clinic in Khartoum will be the first project to be built. His wife, a radiologist, believes that many African women are unaware of the symptoms and are often too shy to come forward for treatment. The clinic, they both hope, will save many lives. 'And no one else is doing it. We are looking for areas like this where we can make a difference.' His wife will base herself there for the first year to help it get off the ground. The couple want to lend their skills as well as their money to their projects. But even here, Mo is concerned to ensure that the clinic will not be completely dependent on his foundation for its running costs. The top two floors of the planned seven-storey building will be high-class offices to be rented out to businesses. Mo is a businessman – good works, like good businesses, he believes, need to be self-supporting if they are to be sustainable in the long run. The clinic will, therefore, also ask for modest contributions from those patients who are able to pay.

His foundation is also looking at education. 'There is so much that needs to be done. Do we focus on the next generation of African leaders, or on elementary education? Do we supply computers and other equipment, or do we train teachers? We have to work out where we can best make a difference and not duplicate what others are doing.' He will.

After thirty years in the UK Mo Ibrahim has come back to Africa, which, in his heart, he has never left. It was, however, a long and eventful journey from Alexandria in Egypt where he grew up, the son of not particularly prosperous middle-class parents from northern Sudan. He graduated at the university there in electrical engineering and started work with the local telecommunications company. Six years later he came to Britain to study for a Masters degree at Bradford on a British Council scholarship and later at Birmingham where he gained his doctorate. He chose mobile communications for his thesis – an unusual and almost unheard-of subject in 1974. It was to be the focus of his work and life for the next thirty years, but it might never have happened had it not been for a taxi ride in Geneva four years earlier. The taxi driver was using a radio phone to talk to his base as he drove along. 'I asked the driver how it worked because, in a city, there is no line of sight between the aerial on the car and the transmitter.' Of course, the driver didn't know, but, back at the International Telecommunications Union where Mo was an intern, it was explained to him that waves scatter, making communication touch and go but allowing some contact. Mo was intrigued, glimpsed the possibilities and decided, there and then, to find out more.

In 1983 he was invited to join British Telecom as technical director of Cellnet, its mobile phone arm and the first such company to be set up in Britain. At that time the technology did not accommodate many customers, so the equipment was very expensive with a total of only 10,000 users in the UK, who were carefully prioritized by the chairman of BT himself. The development of cellular technology changed all that, by allowing many different people to use the same part of the radio spectrum frequency at the same time. This was Mo's speciality and he designed the first cellular operation in the UK, which went into service in 1985. He was lucky, he said, the right person in the right place at the right time. He is being modest.

At that time the phones were accurately called carphones; they operated from bulky equipment carried in the boot of a car with an aerial on the roof and were marketed as car accessories. 'Mobile' referred to the car, not the phone. In 1984 Mo was visiting the United States and at Motorola the engineers showed him a prototype of a phone with a battery that could be held in the hand. It was called a hand-portable. 'I saw at once that this new system need not be based on the car. When I came back I proposed to my bosses at BT that the design of our system should be changed to be based on the hand-portable phones, which meant almost doubling the investment. To their great credit they agreed. Motorola built a production line for us that produced 5,000 phones. We bought all of them, just for London in the first instance, and so, in 1985, London

# Peter Lampl

In the mid-1990s Peter Lampl left the US to return to England where he had grown up, been educated and started work. He came back seriously rich, having set up his own private equity firm, the Sutton Company, in 1983. After a rocky start, the Sutton Company had become a roaring success, as Peter and his partners acquired, improved and successfully exited thirteen companies in four different industries in the States and Europe, turned them round and sold them on. That sounds easy but it requires the skill to know what to do with a business, the management experience to persuade others to do something, and the courage to take a risk. These were all qualities he had acquired in ten years of working first for the Boston Consulting Group and then as president of the real estate division of International Paper, the largest landowner in the world.

But after fourteen years the business of making even more money had lost its appeal. He was, as the saying goes, ready for the beach. 'I was going to play golf and manage my portfolio.' He was forty-nine years old.

Two years year later he woke up to find himself filling most of the front page of *The Times*. 'We were really mortified. All hell broke loose. I had people calling up wanting me to go on radio, television and all that stuff. Two things then happened. The Inland Revenue rang up; it had found out that I had some money. Then my tax adviser called to say that I was now high profile and that I had better talk to Control Risks about security!' He had been outed – as an educational visionary.

It was goodbye to the quiet life. The *Times* article had been written by its education correspondent, who was interested in Peter's ideas and schemes for encouraging and helping the underprivileged young to gain their proper share of Britain's higher education. Peter Lampl, soon to be Sir Peter Lampl, was by then fully engaged in a new career as a full-time and very active educational philanthropist. Publicity, however, was something he neither sought nor wanted. 'I was madder than hell at *The Times*', he says, 'but then I realized that this was something quite powerful. It gets you noticed. Now we try to manage it.'

It is doubtful whether he would ever have been satisfied with golf and money management because his American experience had already stirred his altruistic instincts. 'If you're lucky enough to make money there, you are expected to give something back,' he comments. Nor was he really likely to let those hard-earned skills of business management linger unused for long. Sticking his finger into other people's business must have become a bit of a habit. But the trigger that started him on his new track came in an unexpected way. His return to England coincided with the Dunblane massacre, where a gunman had walked into a Scottish primary school and shot dead a teacher and sixteen children. 'Having lived in America, I felt strongly that handguns were not a good idea, so I contacted the people setting up the Snowdrop campaign on gun control and offered to pay their expenses. The next thing I knew I had the father of a girl shot at the school in my living room.'

The campaign led to a speedy ban on handguns and to Peter's realization that one individual can help to make a difference to a whole society. So when, later that year, he went back to visit his old school in Reigate, where he had been a pupil in the 1960s, and found it a very different place, his urge to do something kicked in. It had been a private school entirely funded by the state. He had gone there at no cost to his parents and his best friend was a farm labourer's son. Now it had gone independent. 'A lot of the kids who had gone there with me wouldn't have been able to go there any more.'

Back at Corpus Christi, the Oxford college where he had studied, things had also changed. 'When I was there two-thirds of Oxford students came from state schools. In the 1990s the proportion had dropped to less than half. I was appalled.' It was, as he saw it, a form of social apartheid. The affluent educated their children privately from nursery school upwards with the result that they seldom mixed with kids from other backgrounds. Most of us would have sighed, lamented the way the educational reforms of the last forty years had turned out, and gone on our way. Peter saw it differently. There were things that could be done, initiatives that he could take that might point the way to remedy what he saw as gross social injustice. And he was a businessman; he knew how to get things done, he understood numbers and valued research, and, later, after his experience with *The Times*, he came to appreciate the difference that the media could make, principally because it gives you leverage with the government.

The first step was to set up his own charity, which he named the Sutton Trust after his old company. He then started by engaging his old university. He suggested to Oxford that he finance and design a two-week summer school at the university for state-school students who came from families with no experience of university education. The purpose would be to correct some of their stereotypes of places like Oxford, to raise their aspirations and to give them the confidence to apply. Oxford was suspicious at first, wary of accepting money from strangers, but was soon convinced by the success of the early programmes. So was the government. Peter used his new media prominence to get to talk to ministers. David Blunkett, then Education Minister, took up the idea of the summer schools. The Sutton Trust and the government now run summer schools at 60 universities for 6,000 inner-city state-school teenagers every year.

Valuable though these schools are, Peter views them as only papering over the cracks in the system. There are, he points out, 3,000 state-school students each year who gain the necessary A-level grades to attend the dozen or so top universities, but who end up elsewhere. In fact, students from the independent sector are as likely to go to one of these prestigious institutions as students from state schools who achieve two grades higher at A level. So more fundamental changes are needed. He embarked on a systematic programme of pilot initiatives, research and campaigning all directed from his modest office in south London.

The next initiative involved Liverpool's independent Belvedere

School for Girls run by the Girls' Public Day School Trust, where the Sutton Trust finances an open access scheme. The trust ensures that the intake is based solely on academic merit. Roughly two-thirds of the girls now come from families with average or below-average earnings. He himself took part in the interview process and is proud of the fact that out of a year group of seventy-two there were fifty-two girls who wouldn't have been able to go there without the help of the trust. After four years of the programme thirty per cent of the girls receive full funding, forty per cent partial funding and the rest pay full fees. The cost of the programme, averaged over all the students, is £3,800 per annum, compared with the cost of £5,000 for the average comprehensive, including capital expenditure. It would, therefore, he argues, be a good deal for the government to fund full open access at 100 or more top independent schools. Given that Britain's independent schools are reckoned to be the best in the world, it only makes sense, he believes, to open them to the best available talent. It might also do away with the snobbery and nepotism that infect such places and make the country more genuinely meritocratic. In the meantime the trust is advocating the extension of the pilot to a further dozen schools.

Peter Lampl likes to target his initiatives on ideas and projects that can then be scaled up with government support. It is what he calls positive intervention. Having attacked the higher end of the educational system he is now turning his attention to the school system. Invited back to his other old school, Pate's Grammar in Cheltenham, he was shocked to find that the school – one of the best in the country – was now virtually the sole preserve of the middle classes. Gone were the bright children from poor backgrounds who were there in his day. The headteacher asked if Peter could help Pate's to address this and reach the less privileged children who live on the council estates that surround the school. The Sutton Trust now funds a full-time outreach officer who works with the 30 primary schools on the estates and runs master classes at the school for 120 students.

Not only does the scheme bring more admissions from these schools but it has also raised awareness among all the schools of the various educational opportunities that are available in the area. There are, his research points out, 200 top performing state schools in the country where free school meals average only 3 per cent compared with the national average of 17 per cent. If the Pate's model were to be adopted at these 200 schools, it would give more reality to the idea of choice in education.

With his American experience Peter Lampl believes there are things we could learn from the other side of the Atlantic. He therefore asked the Boston Consulting Group to look into the possibility of introducing a national network of yellow school buses to the UK. Its research showed that the benefits of yellow buses for primary schools – in terms of less wasted time for parents and commuters, fewer road deaths and injuries, and less congestion and environmental damage – totalled some £458 million a year, set against a cost of just £184 million. The added advantage, from Peter's point of view, is that an expanded network of dedicated school buses would give more young people, particularly from less affluent homes, access to better schools, which are often too far from their homes if their parents don't have cars and the time to drive them there.

The other American idea worth copying, he believes, is the SAT basis of university admissions. This test measures aptitude and would be a valuable adjunct to A-level scores, identifying those whose abilities had not shown up in their grades. The Sutton Trust funded two trials of the test by the National Foundation for Educational Research, and Peter himself, as a member of the Schwartz Committee on university admissions, successfully argued for its inclusion in the committee's report.

The last eight years have been busy. 'I'm fascinated by this stuff,' he says. 'I probably work fifty hours a week at least on it. I'm not retired!' Nor is there any sign of him slowing down in the near future, although with two young children he has his own responsibilities as a parent. He pumps £3 million of his own money into the trust every year but would now like to see it boosted by funds from elsewhere, given the amount of work that is crying out for attention.

You have to wonder where his passion comes from. His Stateside experience clearly affected him. He was, as he says, very conscious of the tradition in that country for the wealthy to give something back to the society where they had flourished and he is clearly pleased to be able to bring some of that spirit back to Britain. Combine that with his business acumen, his desire for action and his ability to get things done by others, and you have a potent mix. But underpinning all these lies his deep concern for social justice and social mobility. Where does it come from? Maybe it owes a little to his ancestry. His father came to Britain in 1938 from Austria at the age of seventeen to escape the Nazis, together with his grand-parents who were originally from Czechoslovakia. After the war his father had to start again from a council estate in Wakefield, where Peter was born. In due course he got his qualifications, became a successful businessman and a director of a public company. His father was bright and determined, but what was possible for his father surely has to be on offer for everyone. Sadly, research the Sutton Trust commissioned shows that social mobility in Britain has declined for those born in the 1970s compared to those born in the 1950s. It has become tougher, not easier, for those at the bottom to get to the top. And even though the absolute number of university places is growing, this expansion has overwhelmingly benefited the middle classes. Sir Peter Lampl is determined to do his best to reverse the trend.

# Chris Mathias

'When I grew up in India in the 1960s and '70s,' says Chris Mathias, 'India was run by a very small group of families, perhaps 1,000, who all knew each other, went to the same schools, belonged to the same clubs, married into each other's families. Then there were 750 million other people. If you were in that small privileged group of the top bankers, industrialists, civil servants and politicians, as my family was, it never struck me as at all unusual. We lived in our own world with guards on the gates, cooks, chauffeurs, servants, horses, swimming, tennis, everything we might need. When I was driven to our very nice school each morning, as the car came out of the gates, I wouldn't notice, wouldn't even see, the people lying in the road, some of whom were literally starving to death. Even though my father kept telling me, it never really struck a chord.'

Chris was sixteen when he left India to come to London in 1977. He remembers driving into London from the airport and being struck by the fact that there were no starving and destitute people, no sick and dying bodies lying by the wayside. 'Suddenly it all fell into place, a lot of things that my father had been trying to make me see began to make sense. It was a real wake-up call. The world doesn't have to be this way.' The seeds of his philanthropy were sown that day. Today, through Digital Links and as trustee of a number of other charities, he is making his own contribution to changing that world, applying the skills and the money he has made in business to meeting social needs in the developing world.

Digital Links International was founded in 2002 in order to help people in the developing world have access to information technology in order to improve their lives. It collects surplus PCs from private and public corporations in the UK, refurbishes them and, with the help of local partners, provides them at low cost to schools, charities or small enterprises in Africa. Chris feels strongly that aid that merely allows the recipients to continue what they are already doing is not helpful. The point is to help them to change, to move into a new world of work and commerce. So Digital Links also trains teachers in IT skills and, to back up the computers it distributes, it is heavily involved in attempts to provide solar and wireless technologies to make connectivity to the internet possible in remote areas. Going further, it has been asked by Britain's Department for International Development to investigate a proposal to use information technology to provide distance learning to train 90,000 teachers and school heads in Kenya.

Digital Links works in Africa, not India. India, Chris says, is a very different land to the one he grew up in. The Indians are now more than able, and increasingly willing, to help themselves, particularly in IT. If Africa can be brought to the same state of capability, the continent might be on the way to solving its own problems. Chris is now, formally, the deputy chairman of the charity, leaving the hard work of implementation to the CEO, David Sogan, and the staff on the ground.

All this was still to come when Chris landed at Heathrow that morning, when he was only sixteen, when the internet was unheard of and computers were still so big they filled a basement. Much was to happen to both Chris and the world in between.

On arrival in Britain he was sent to a small Catholic boarding school in Plymouth, where he claims to be the only pupil ever to have been expelled. 'I hate rules, unless I know why.' he says. When he went for his interview at Bristol University his interviewer told him that he had never read a worse reference from a head teacher. 'I have been so looking forward to meeting you, you must be so bad,' the professor said. 'I knew, as soon as I saw the reference, that we would give you a place.' It was Chris's initiation into both the pitfalls and the fruits of doing things his own way, of his latent entrepreneurship. He studied Development Economics at Bristol, a taste of things to come, but decided that a job in the World Bank was not for him – too bureaucratic, too full of career professionals. Instead he worked for Arthur Andersen to get a work permit and to learn accountancy, before gaining an MBA at INSEAD, the business school in Fontainebleau, and coming back to London to join Bain, the management consultants.

'I loved Bain, but it was a totally mercenary decision to join them. They paid me an awful lot of money and I had a huge loan to pay off.' That loan was twice what it needed to be because, having secured a loan of some £37,000 to finance his studies, Chris put it all on some call options, hoping to double his money in a rising market. Unfortunately, he did it the week before Black Monday in October 1987 when the markets collapsed and his £37,000 dwindled, in one day, to £2,000. He went back to his bank managers, who generously lent him enough to complete his MBA. It was one more lesson in risk and opportunity.

He was soon to apply that lesson for real when he joined a venture capital funded company and was given the responsibility for turning it around, which he did sucessfully. 'I made my boss the 233rd richest man in the United Kingdom, according to the *Sunday Times* Rich List,' he comments. He bought himself a red Ferrari. 'Looking back, my hair stands on end at some of the things I did. I turned up one day to fire 250 workers – in my new bright red Ferrari.' His only excuse was that he was just twenty-eight and incredibly naïve.

During this meteoric early career he met rejection only once. He asked Claire, whom he had known and loved for seven years, to seal their relationship by marrying him. She said, 'No. I love you but you don't know where you are going.' It was probably something he needed to hear. Stunned, he thought of leaving Britain and wandering around the world. Instead, he listened to a friend, went to INSEAD and began to sort out his future. Next time he wooed her she said yes.' Just as well, because her advice was soon to prove crucial to his future. Having achieved two successful turnarounds for others, he decided to go for broke and do the same on his own. Claire was willing. 'All right,' she said, 'I'll back you, and if it all goes wrong I won't give you any grief, but there is one caveat – you must take Martin Gill as your partner.' Martin was an old friend and, says Chris, 'quite the opposite to me, meticulous, conscientious, disciplined'. Martin accepted, and the rest, you could say, is history.

'That was the end of my education,' Chris says. 'Now my business career started for real.' They bought a 140-year-old envelope manufacturing company and turned it round, then sold it on. At about the same time, in 1991, he had started Conduit Communications, which was to be the financial base for his future. It was the very beginning of the laptop age. 'What happens,' Chris asked himself, 'when computers are powerful, ubiquitous and communicating not computing? The world will change.' He set himself the task of working out what the impact of this change would be. 'Then the internet came along and how lucky were we!' Conduit set out to help companies cope with these revolutionary changes. There were, at that time, only two real competitors in Europe. Conduit grew and grew and grew, at 100 per cent per annum from 1993 to 2000, ending up with well over 100 staff. Then he was made an offer he couldn't refuse and sold the company. In the meantime he and Martin had not been idle. They had bought, put in new management, turned around and sold five other companies. He was rich. 'I love making money, I have to be honest. It's playing tennis for real.'

It was, however, the start of a new century and for Chris, a new life stage. He was forty. 'I wanted to help make the world a better place. I have always given money to charity, yet I wanted to *do* something that would make a difference. But I was an amateur. I needed to go back to school.' However, there wasn't anything like a business school for would-be development philanthropists. He linked up with Oxfam and ActionAid and started funding some of their projects, which helped him to get his feet on the ground. He joined the boards of some other charities, and after two busy years he was no longer a well-meaning amateur. 'At the very least, nobody could pull the wool over my eyes any more.'

Given his experience of introducing businesses to the communication age it is not that surprising that he was excited by the thought of doing something similar, even if more basic, for the next generation in the developing world. Combine that with the fact that 3 million PCs in this country go into landfill every year, and the seeds of Digital Links were there. There were, of course, already many small initiatives taking discarded computers and distributing them to African schools, 'but I wanted to do it on a large scale so that we would have a significant effect. I found a couple of African operations to support, but there is a lot of distrust between voluntary bodies and business, so I decided to set up Digital Links.'

He persuaded Bain to investigate the possibilities. Its consultants did ten months of work for free and came back recommending that it was a viable proposition. 'That support was very important. In business I knew what I was doing. In this development work I was very unsure of what to do, so the help and support of my colleague Jo Bell was crucial, as was her belief in the idea.' Also important was the early help from Barclays Bank. Chris dates the real beginning of Digital Links to a dinner in Monte Carlo when he, with the help of his companions, sold the idea to the chairman of Barclays, Matthew Barrett. As soon as that happened Chris brought in David Sogan as CEO to get it moving. Barclays had responded magnificently, staff cleaned their old computers, packed them up and delivered them to the docks ready for shipping. 'They were wonderful, because we had no infrastructure at the time, we had nothing. These days we charge to collect and clean and we charge at the other end. We are now self-supporting. It was about eighteen months until we reached cash break-even. We don't want to have to beg.'

Digital Links is now up and running, very actively. Chris is still doing business; he loves the game, as he says, and is obviously good at it. But he is also a family man, with three daughters and a very special wife who runs the family and all its concerns, as well as chairing the local branch of Home-Start. The family's memory box is, he says, probably the most important object in his still life. He is also, of course, an Indian and very proud of it and his heritage. He keeps the Buddha statue to remind him not just of India, but that material things are not the way to measure yourself. The more spiritual aspects of life cannot be measured by others. Only you can know what is good and right. For Chris one of those immeasurable things is his love of horses and of riding. A shy, asthmatic, reclusive boy, he changed into a confident, fit, outgoing teenager when he started to ride. He hasn't stopped since and plays polo regularly. 'The trust between horse and rider,' he says, 'is amazing, and that horse in the still life was given to me by Martin Gill, another example of absolute trust. I treasure my watch, too, because it was what Claire gave me on our wedding day. None of this would have happened without her. But it also reminds me that time is so precious. At forty you know you won't live for ever. You can plan as much as you can but in the end you have to seize the moment or you end up planning for ever.' And the flower? 'That's Claire's favourite, and it's pretty I love beautiful things. All my horses are pretty.'

A busy man, therefore, but nowadays someone who very clearly knows where he is going and, on past evidence, is likely to get there

## Still Life

Memory box – the family
Buddha – India and spirituality
Horse – riding and trust
Baseball cap – Conduit Communications
Watch – Claire, time is precious
Bougainvillea – beauty and Claire's favourite.

# Fred Matser

Fred Matser was thirty-seven when his life changed. The son of a businessman, and by that time a successful one himself, he was also a humanitarian at heart who yearned for wider horizons and the chance to serve humanity more directly. Triggered into action by his experiences at a Young Presidents' Organization conference, he moved with his family to Switzerland to fulfil a boyhood dream of working for the Red Cross, where he held the voluntary position of executive chairman of the Child Alive programme for three years. 'I had no need of money,' he says. 'I just wanted to help and empower others.' Since then he has founded or co-founded over fifteen foundations spanning the fields of healthcare, the environment, conservation and peace. 'I discovered once that the word "Fred" means peace in Swedish,' he says, with quiet satisfaction, for it became his life's work to inspire and enable others to work for a more functional and peaceful world. For this work he received the Van Emden Prize in Holland in 1995 and the International Caring Award in 1992 in Washington, DC.

Fred was the third child in a family of five, although, sadly, two of the brothers died. His father was an entrepreneur, a self-made and self-taught man who started the first independent property development business in the Netherlands. He was, says Fred, 'a really great man', a man of vision, highly intelligent and courageous who loved his work and was very altruistic, but who lived in the same modest house all his life. The family routine, as Fred recalls it, was simple, almost austere – eggs only on Sunday, just one slice of cheese on their bread, with the boys using the girls' bathwater to bath in. Not a bad preparation for life, he now thinks. Indeed, he has clearly inherited many of his father's attitudes and aptitudes, managing to be a successful businessman as well as an adventurous and visionary social entrepreneur, while still maintaining a fairly modest profile and way of life.

When Fred was nineteen his father, who was suffering badly from diabetes and Parkinson's Disease, told his son that he would like him to be the one who took over the business. 'I was flabbergasted,' says Fred, 'I was not the businessman. That was my younger brother, Paul. I wanted to study. I reluctantly agreed, however, on condition that after a year I could move out if I wanted to.' But after the year was up he was too involved to be able to leave. At twenty-three he became secretary to the board, joined it at twenty-five and two years later, became chairman. His father died five years later. By then the business had expanded to employ nearly 200 people, including staff in its subsidiary companies, developing and running shopping centres, housing estates, an insurance business and infrastructural works. By then, too, Fred had married and fathered three children, and was proud of running a profitable business with integrity and honesty, something not too common, he says, among his competitors at the time.

In 1980 came that fateful YPO conference where he saw Yuri Geller bend spoons and make broken clocks start ticking, 'even the key to my front door was bent so that I could not use it any more,' and where he met a psychic called Greta Woodrow who startled him by revealing things about him and his past that no one could have known. It was Fred's first taste of the paranormal, of the world beyond our senses. 'Am I in control of my own life?' he began to wonder, 'or is there something else that I don't understand?' Greta had warned him and many others that the world was facing a cataclysm and that he should consider moving to a faraway place like Australia or to a mountainous land. He was ready to move on anyway, but the fear of a cataclysm precipitated his move. After looking at Australia he chose Switzerland and the Red Cross.

Five million children under five die every year of dehydration caused by diarrhoea, he learnt, when he was asked to chair the Child Alive programme that the Red Cross was about to establish to tackle the problem. A very simple mixture of salt, sugar and water that can be administered by any member of the family will, in 90 per cent of cases, keep the sufferer alive. He and his team were asked to launch a worldwide rehydration programme using this formula. So often, he observes, business ignores the simple and the natural because the complicated solution will be more profitable. Launched on his new career, Fred found a successor to run the real estate business in Holland, going back just once a month to check on progress.

It was at this time that he began to have several of what might best be called out-of-body experiences and began to develop his philosophy of life and well-being. The finite world of time and space, he believes, is the expression of the infinite. The infinite is to do with our being rather than our doing. In his own life he has tried to combine the two and the chief purpose of his philanthropic endeavours is to give people more control over their health and personal development. Philanthropy that aims to solve people's problems for them breeds dependency, he feels, and is not sustainable in the long run. Lasting improvement, he believes, only happens when individuals take a personal stake in the outcome and take on what he calls their own responsAbility.

Some clues as to what drives him can be found in his still life. The stone, a crystal, symbolizes his connection to the infinite, to what lies beyond and above the material world. He uses the crystal in his regular meditations. The carving of two hands is a gift from his friend Jerry Jampolsky, who gave it to Fred when he returned from Israel, where he had been trying to work for peace. Fred keeps it in his bedroom. 'I lie in bed and see the light shining through it. It symbolizes the male and the female, but also God and prayer, and it reminds me of my old friend and his lifelong work. It stands for friendship and peace.'

war? 'The idea came to me that I should gather together as many gold medal winners as possible and bring them to Sarajevo. After many negotiations with the United Nations and other bodies, I got a plane from the Dutch Ministry of Defence and flew in thirteen gold medal winners from all over the world. We made the statement that we had not forgotten the people of Sarajevo.' Afterwards, lengthy discussions led eventually, in 2003, to the erection of a Peace Flame House in Tuzla, a lovely building, he says, based, once more, on organic architecture with a 100-capacity auditorium and rooms for therapy.

Then there was the joint project that he engineered with Mikhail Gorbachev. Hearing that the Russian government wanted help to build a transplant clinic for children and was appealing for half of the $2 million cost, he pledged half a million dollars from his own resources. Having met the former Soviet president at a breakfast function in New York and later, at Gorbachev's invitation, in Moscow, Fred persuaded him to match it from his speaking tour earnings in the US.

Fred has gone on to invest in micro-credit systems in Uganda and the Philippines in conjunction with Muhammad Yunus and is, along with others, currently looking at Jeffrey Sachs's Millennium Villages Project. As far as possible, he says, he tries to work with other partners because it brings forth more joy to do things together.

Fred is now sixty, but his energy seems undiminished after more than twenty years of seeking to inspire and empower others. Just as well, since the world is full of places and people who need his work.

## Still Life

Crystal – the infinite
Two hands – peace, harmony between opposites
Torch – light and love
Shoe – the Earth and gravity
Ring – love and family
Hyacinth – early memories

# Niall Mellon

In 2004 Niall Mellon chartered a plane and flew 343 volunteer Irish workmen to Imizamo Yethu, a township outside Cape Town. There thcy built 50 new three-bedroom houses in under a week to replace just some of the shacks that the 14,000 inhabitants called home. This meant that 350 of those who lived in that shanty town would have a proper home of their own in time for Christmas. In 2005 Niall upped the numbers, bringing out 500 workers who built 106 new breeze-block houses in two weeks. He has ambitions to see all 2.3 million shacks in South Africa's townships replaced by proper homes in time for the football World Cup in 2010 that will be held there and will do his best to make it happen. It was, you might think, an odd thing for a 37-year-old property developer from Dublin to do, particularly since no one asked him to do it, but then Niall Mellon has never conformed to any pattern.

He started selling fire extinguishers door to door, using money he was given at his confirmation at the age of thirteen. He had mixed success but, he recalls, 'One man told me that I was a better salesman than anyone in his business and told me to give him a call when I left school.' As Niall says, one early word of praise can set you up for life. He knew then that he had some skills, even though he later left school at seventeen with low grades – except in two business subjects. He was a self-made millionaire by the age of twenty-four and now runs a large property development company, Earthquake, building apartment complexes in Ireland and Britain.

In 2002 he bought a second home in Hout Bay outside Cape Town. On his visits there he often walked past the township that cluttered the side of the valley directly opposite where the rich white folk lived. The contrast reinforced his wish to play some part in building the new South Africa. 'I feel that if South Africa succeeds there is hope for the whole continent.' He wondered then what it might be like to live in a place like Imizamo Yethu. He had been warned by rich South Africans, both black and white, that it would be extremely dangerous for him to get involved.

Ignoring their advice, he went into the township one day and was, he said, humbled by the welcome he received. He asked to meet the leaders. He would, he said, like to contribute in some way to the township, perhaps by building houses. But the community leaders asked for help with education, not housing. They had people, they said, who were qualified to go to college but lacked the money. So Niall provided sponsorship for twenty-five young people to go on vocational courses, from secretarial to engineering to biochemistry. 'That was the start of my involvement,' he says.

But housing was still on his mind. He discovered that this community, with 14,000 people, had only built six proper houses in the last ten years. He proposed that he and the community join forces to create a partnership to build more houses. 'I wanted to put myself on the same level as the people there, so it had to be a partnership.' In the first weeks he had around 100 willing workers. He paid them the going rate, the equivalent of about £68 a month for a labourer, and came back every two weeks or so from Europe to see what was happening. He found, disappointingly, that production halved when he wasn't there. So he divided the workers into seven teams who would only be paid on the completion of each house. A little ruefully, he says, 'I readjusted my plan in the light of experience.'

This work continues. Phase One consists of 450 houses of which almost all have now been built and he hopes to complete 700-plus in Phase Two and then to move on to other townships. When he is in Ireland Niall is on the phone most days to his foreman in South Africa. The houses are sold to their future occupants for an average price of £3,400, but Niall offers them all an interest-free mortgage over 14 years and requires the future owner to work for him for 300 hours for free. When the money is repaid it is ploughed back into more developments. Yes, they would love to be given a free home and, Niall says, 'Ninety-five per cent of me would like to give them the houses, but if they have to sweat and pay for them then they really take a pride in their ownership.' Even with these generous terms many of the occupants find it difficult to make the repayments. It was, he said, really difficult to explain the idea of a mortgage to these people. 'For many it isn't the choice between a night out and making the repayments, it is between buying food and making repayments.' Niall has had to extend some of the mortgages to twenty-five years and may yet have to write off a few of the outstanding balances.

Niall put €1 million of his own money into the project to get it going, and has since raised a further €3 million, but his real contribution is his time: every week or ten days he goes out there to work for two or three days. He has, he agrees, a very understanding wife. His next step, however, was going to demand even more of his time and energy. It was in 2003 that he decided to involve more of his fellow Irishmen in his venture.

'I had two objectives with the Irish volunteer trips. Building more houses was one of them, but there was another. Ireland has bene-fited enormously from the Celtic Tiger economy. Some have not prospered but many are now millionaires. There is a new generation growing up who have no memory of recession or of difficult times. We have to demonstrate to those countries that haven't yet got as far as Ireland that one of the key parameters of success is giving something back to people who need our help.' He has said that he was initially worried that Ireland was becoming a selfish country, but his experience with his volunteer trips has changed that view. 'Both giver and receiver have benefited. All the volunteers have been touched by meeting real people who live in these conditions.'

The volunteers, many of them qualified craftspeople but some offering only their labour, have to raise €5,000 each to cover their travel and living expenses and to contribute to the cost of the houses they will build. Niall has been surprised and delighted both by the numbers volunteering and by the imaginative ways they raised the money for the trip – bingo nights, marathons, soccer matches, race nights, even inviting a transvestite to live on their building site for a week.

The first year he recruited 150 volunteers. In 2004 there were nearly 350. The visits had to be very well organized because when 350 people arrive off a plane and start work within a few hours there are a lot of things to be arranged in advance. 'I couldn't do it on my own. I need the help of those six or seven volunteers who come out a couple of days earlier to put it all in place.' Niall makes it all sound simple, but the feat of bringing a motley assortment of volunteer workers to a strange country and building fifty houses in a week requires organizational skills of a high order, as well as the vision of a leader even to think of it in the first place. There are the qualities Niall demonstrates in his 'day job', where he has also had the courage and vision to go where no one else was going. It is, in a way, just more of the same, but this time for the benefit of the poor not the rich.

He says that the symbolic value of a plane-load of volunteers coming from a little island 6,000 miles away to work twelve hours a day can't be underestimated. 'Maybe 50 million people in Africa watched a piece of those volunteers working in the township that week.' The downside for Niall personally has been that he has had to shed his low profile in order to promote his Township Challenge. He is, in fact, probably better known in South Africa than in Ireland and was fortunate to be given office space in Mandela's private office. He has used his profile there and his friendship with Mandela to urge South Africans to commit themselves to building those 2.3 million homes that are needed to replace all the shacks by the time of the 2010 World Cup.

'I suggested a number of practical ways in which the housing programme could be accelerated, like the setting up of a supreme housing authority that could grant immediate and unchallengeable permission, a process that could take years off the process. I think that the Irish Township project has given people a great motivation to get things like this done.' Ultimately, however, the provision of proper housing is the responsibility of the South African government, but it could, Niall believes, do a lot just by disentangling the layers of bureaucracy.

Niall has come a long way from his early beginnings as one of five kids in what he describes as a close but thrifty family, although there has been a hint of a connection to a possible forebear in the distant past who was far from poor. He treasures his copy of the private diary of Thomas Mellon, who started as a labourer in Ireland, went on to become the richest man in America in the nineteenth century and ended up as the first great American philanthropist before his death in 1908. Niall tells how, one day, a man walked into his father's shop with the book and, pointing to a photograph of Mellon, said to his father, 'That man looks just like you.'

Whether there was a connection there or only a coincidence, one thing was certain – the wealth of Thomas Mellon never reached the Irish Mellon family, which was one reason why Niall grew up determined to make money. He started early with his fire extinguishers. On leaving school he moved into a job with a bank that only made him more determined to be self-employed. He left and set himself up as an investment adviser at the age of eighteen. He is proud that he moved his clients into cash the day before the markets crashed in 1987, but he failed to anticipate the invasion of Kuwait, which caused the markets to fall twenty per cent overnight.

He switched careers after that, became a mortgage broker and formed a federation of the leading mortgage brokers in Ireland, believing that acting together they would have more clout. He was elected chairman at twenty-four. In 1992 the Irish property market was on its knees. Niall persuaded a number of investors to join him in taking a long-term view, betting that the market would eventually turn up again. It did. 'That made a lot of people wealthy,' he says, including himself. He kept his head down for the next twelve years while he expanded his property interests, first in Ireland then in Britain. Some say he is now worth some hundreds of millions of euros. He doesn't say, perhaps he doesn't know. The money itself seems to be of little interest to him except for the things it enables him to do. 'Money has its limitations. It can be a noose around your neck.' And it carries obligations. 'I don't want to be too heavy about it, but I do believe that if you are successful you should give something back. If you do it in your lifetime, you get to enjoy the difference it makes.' Perhaps, too, the diary of Thomas Mellon, with his views on life, had an influence. 'To this day I have never read a book that has had as big an impact on me. His ideology is identical to mine.' Is he religious then, perhaps? 'Not particularly,' he says. It is in trees, flowers and nature that he finds peace, renewal and a reminder of what endures in life.

Most would call him successful beyond the norm. But success, in his view, should be a balance of things. That balance was changed for him at age thirty-five when he married, buying a top hat especially for the occasion, and then by the birth of his son. These were new and important commitments. 'I have a very successful business,' he says, 'but I want to be almost out of it in three years and to devote the next ten years to fulfilling my life in a much more balanced way.' It seems certain, however, that Africa will long remain a significant part of that new balance. That is one place where he can really make a difference, and already has.

## Still Life

Diary of Thomas Mellon – a model for life
African sculpture – Africa
Painting – the Township Challenge
Top hat – marriage and commitment
Dummy – his baby son, the future
Tree flower – a love of nature

# Daniel Petre

One morning in 1992, aged just thirty-two, Daniel Petre was gearing himself up to make a presentation to Bill Gates and a dozen of the top executives of Microsoft at Gates's summer property on Hood Canal outside Seattle. He paused for just a moment to marvel at how he had come to be there, the youngest vice-president in Microsoft, an Australian, one of only two non-Americans in that group that morning, married to Carolyn and with a daughter, Grace, born before they left Australia two years before. Success, he said to himself, doesn't get much better than this, not at thirty-two.

Then in December that year came the telephone call. It was his mother phoning from Australia with the worst of news. Daniel's sister Gabriela, whom he dearly loved, had been killed in a car crash between Canberra and Young. She left behind a baby girl, badly injured, and a husband, also hurt. Life, he immediately realized, was not as controllable as he had assumed up until then. To have something so valuable as his sister's life taken away so suddenly, without any warning, without the discussion or the workshopping or the decision-making processes that had preceded all the other major events in his working life, was truly shocking, he says. To be unable to exchange all the tokens of his success for a simple telephone call with his sister was traumatizing. His life and his priorities, he discovered, were about to change.

Today he is one of Australia's leading philanthropists with his own pioneering foundation. But his concern for society does not stop with his cheques, useful though they are. He is a philanthropist with a mission. He wants nothing less than to change the meaning of success in modern society.

Success, he feels, is too narrowly defined, particularly in the corporate world. Money, status, social recognition too often take priority over the needs of the family. That is bad for the family, particularly the children, bad for communities and, ultimately, bad for the individual.

The trigger point for him came when his brother-in-law consulted him about the words to go on Gabriela's tombstone. Still in Seattle at the time, he realized that if he were to die then himself all that could be put on his stone would be 'Vice-President of Microsoft', not at all bad in itself but not enough to justify a life, he felt. He knew then that he had to return to Australia to be with his family and to help his sister's husband and tiny daughter. Bill Gates was sympathetic and moved the Asia Pacific headquarters of Microsoft from Seattle to Australia and put Daniel in charge.

Back in Australia he worked for Microsoft for four hectic years, then for Kerry Packer's ecorp Ltd for another five, before deciding he at last had the money that he needed for his foundation as well as enough to live on. He could now give his time to his real concern, the need to rebalance individual priorities in life to get a better balance between career, family and community. It was the start of his own personal campaign, one to which he now gives a lot of his energy and a great deal of passion. It began with a book, *Father Time*, published in 1998. *Father Time* had a simple message: people who have taken the decision to become fathers should *be* fathers. This means that they should spend *real* time with their children and family, not just 'quality time' that euphemism for rationed time. They should organize their lives so that they are at home to eat with their kids on, maybe, three evenings a week, should try not to work at weekends, should go to school with their children for a morning once a term and, in general, give their family priority over their work when the two collide – because the family is more important.

It was, he thought, an uncontroversial message. How wrong he was! He was viewed as a traitor to his executive class; he had touched a raw nerve in Australian corporate life. Daniel tells how at one work function a large aggressive man, the managing partner in a law firm, stormed up to him.

'You don't understand,' this man said, 'all this family-time stuff is bullshit.'

'Pardon?'

'You don't understand the responsibilities I shoulder. You don't understand how much I am needed. I can't go fishing with my son.'

'So you don't have any discretionary time? Do you ever take time for a corporate golf day?'

'Of course I do. How else do I get to know people and to find out what is going on in the industry?'

'Come on,' said Daniel, 'we both know that those things are not 100 per cent productive, that they use a lot of time to achieve not very much.'

It was then, Daniel reports, that the lawyer lost his temper.

Daniel became the public target for every dissatisfied executive with high blood pressure. He was seen as attacking the whole value system of the corporate world. 'It was vitriolic,' he says now. At public and social occasions he would be viciously attacked by people who claimed that they couldn't possibly do what he was saying without damaging their business or job. It was, they insinuated, all very well for him, someone who was rich enough to have the time to give to his other interests including his family. It wasn't always like that, however. When he arrived in Seattle to work with Microsoft he encountered the famous Microsoft culture where the running joke was that at Microsoft you only worked half-time – you just had to decide which twelve hours of the day you wanted to work.

The cafeteria was open all day long every day of the year. The

one wonders, does he get his very obvious energy and entrepreneurial spirit? Not from his father, it seems. His parents came to Australia from Romania and Daniel says that his father, who had been a professor of philosophy in his home country, never really settled, never understood his son or recognized his achievements, and is now living out his last days back in Europe. Perhaps it came from his mother, who built a successful fashion design business from scratch in Sydney. His parents divorced when Daniel was sixteen and it may be their experience that has led to Daniel's deep commitment to family life and, especially, to his own wife and family, which now consists of three daughters. Perhaps, too, the Pathways to Manhood project is a testament to Daniel's failure to connect with his own father. He had, he says, to find his own way in life, to light his own path, but now he would like to do the same for others, if he can. If you know what's truly important, he says, life becomes beautifully simple.

'I'm not sure what project comes next,' Daniel says, 'and I worry what effect all this exposure I get will have on my children.' But you sense that he is not going to stop. 'I think I am well positioned to be the heretic on the fringe.' It is a role he obviously enjoys – and does well.

## Still Life

Football – childhood sport, teams and mutual help
Camera – to capture memories of the family
Ring – marriage, commitment and trust
Watch – time is precious, balance
Torch – lighting the way, for self and others
Frangipani – truth is beauty, simplicity as the key to life

# Christopher and Phillida Purvis

Christopher and Phillida Purvis are an unusual couple. They both gave up their main income-producing jobs in their forties in order to concentrate all their energies on their charitable enthusiasms. Christopher describes how it happened:

'One Sunday evening I calculated my assets on the back of an envelope and I said to Phillida, "We don't need to earn any money again." I had never sought to make any money. I was in Japan at the right time and it just sort of happened. If I had known that, just as I was walking out, the stock market was about to collapse, I might not have done it. But I have no regrets, absolutely none. I had a vague idea that I was not going to do very much, that after a leisurely breakfast I would get into my car and go and see a nice church in Suffolk, but, of course, I haven't done that once!'

Instead, in a meeting with the Japanese Ambassador to Britain, he found himself proposing himself as the unpaid chief executive of Japan 2001, a major cultural festival in the UK. He is now on the board of successor charities encouraging mutual understanding between Japan and Britain.

For twenty-three years before that momentous evening he had been working as an investment banker with Warburgs, first in London, then in Japan. It was here that his passion for the Japanese culture was first kindled and where he met Phillida, who was then working for the British Diplomatic Corps and who, later, after they had married, studied at Tokyo University as a postgraduate.

Christopher and Phillida have now built up a formidable collection of charitable activities to which they contribute their time, managerial skills and enthusiasm. They might best be described as portfolio philanthropists, spreading their time and energy across a range of organizations rather than rationing themselves to just one project or cause. Most of the money their ventures need has to be raised from elsewhere, as their own wealth is what allows them to devote so much time to philanthropy while they still have four children at school.

Their one joint entrepreneurial venture springs from their shared love of Japan. They are working together to create the Japan Arena of which Christopher is chairman and Phillida chief executive. This will be a centre in London for all things Japanese, a place where, they hope, people will come to sample the food as well as the culture, art, sport and business experience of that country and, especially, its non-profit community organizations, something of particular concern to Phillida. The Arena will house restaurants as well as social entrepreneurs and some businesses to add the buzz of the profit-making world. Christopher's work for Anglo-Japanese relations was recognized by the award of a CBE in 2002 and by the Japanese Foreign Minister's Commendation, and Phillida's contribution by an MBE in 2004.

Phillida is a serial social entrepreneur. She will pick up an idea and run with it. She had been deputy director of the Daiwa Anglo-Japanese Foundation, where she developed projects that brought the two countries closer together. On leaving the foundation to become a full-time philanthropist she started her own project, founding Links Japan, which promotes exchanges between organizations in the non-profit sectors of Britain and Japan so that both can learn from each other. She started the UK–Japan Dialogue to bring the NGOs of each country together to share experiences and later created a set of links between communities in both nations. She was joint founder of the Burma Campaign Society which aims to foster reconciliation between the veterans of Britain and Japan's encounter in World War Two. On top of these she is a director of the Global Links Initiative, a global network of social entrepreneurs with a special focus on China and Japan, a trustee of the International Refugee Trust, a committee member of the Japan Society as well as a council member of Gap Activity Projects, which sends young people from around the world to volunteer in community projects in other countries.

Christopher, on the other hand, has opportunities thrust upon him, including, most particularly, Handel House, because, in addition to Japan, Christopher's other great passion is music. He first got involved with London's Handel House Museum, at 25 Brook Street where Handel lived and worked, when he was asked to join its board shortly before he left Warburgs. It is, he says, one of the most important artist's houses anywhere in the world and it was falling down. He was asked to take charge of the restoration and it reopened in 2001. He remains deeply involved with it as its chairman. He is also chairman of the Academy of Ancient Music, where his financial and management experience and contacts have proved their value in his new world of philanthropic governance. To these he has added a raft of other concerns. At last count his portfolio contained twelve philanthropic activities, including sitting on the boards of the Royal Academy of Music, a number of other music charities and two grant-giving foundations. He also takes an active role in his local community centre, with a particular involvement in its project to help young people to aspire to and prepare themselves for university.

Where did this passion for music come from? 'It started in my teens. I was always dashing off to London from my boarding school to see the opera at Covent Garden and to enjoy the excitement of those great performances; so much so that my housemaster once wryly observed that it would be nice if I spent some time at the school. Later, I remember, I bought the full set of the records of

# Gordon Roddick

In 1991 Gordon Roddick was in New York, doing business on behalf of the Body Shop, the innovative and socially conscious business that he and his wife Anita had founded and were then running. 'I was near Grand Central Station one afternoon and I saw a large black man selling a newspaper, but he seemed quite animated so I went over to him and asked him what he was doing. He explained that he was homeless and was selling that paper to get some money. He said that it made him feel a part of society, like a human being again, because he was involved in a commercial relationship with the public, rather than asking for a handout. He said it had changed his life. I felt it was a brilliant idea.' Gordon came back to London, where homelessness was then a major problem. He rang John Bird. 'I knew he could write, he had been in the printing and publishing business, and we had had a little flurry of business experiences together. I trusted him 100 per cent. I knew that if there was one person who could make this work it was him.'

I told him, 'You've got to research it and do it, because I think it's a great idea and I will somehow find the money to finance it.' So John did, and Gordon financed what became the *Big Issue* through his company's foundation.

It was the first of a string of 'social businesses' that Gordon has helped to found, finance and support. His and Anita's commitment to social and environmental change through business was the driving force behind the Body Shop from its conception, and since Gordon stepped down as co-chairman in 2002, he has taken his concerns into other spheres. A social business is a commercially run company that is designed to create a social benefit. The *Big Issue* magazine is a traditional business that provides an occupation for people facing homelessness. Around 50 per cent of the turnover goes to the vendors on the streets with any surplus profits going, not to shareholders, but to the Big Issue Foundation charity. Social businesses are a new and growing form of philanthropy, but even the more traditional of charitable donors would ideally like to see the object of their charity become self-supporting and therefore self-sustaining.

Gordon believes however, that it is not that easy to take a charity and make it run as a business. It is easier to do it the other way round, to take the business model and make it work for the social good. Typically, these social businesses require an initial philanthropic invest-ment of money or a guarantee of a bank loan or overdraft to get them started, along with a healthy dose of realism to balance their dreams. It also just so happens that this is what Gordon is good at, after all those years running the business side of the Body Shop, but with his attention also focused on creating social good of some kind.

Gordon does not personally run these social businesses, even the ones that he has himself instigated or inspired. He remains resolutely behind the scenes as a very involved investor, not seeking a conven-tional return on his investment but wanting to ensure that it is being put to proper use. 'My heart is there,' he says, as well as his money. He may, on occasion, take a seat on their boards, but even when he doesn't, as with the Big Issue Foundation now, he rides hard on the management, offering tough support. 'I hover above them like a peregrine falcon.' In that sense he is a venture philanthropist. The difference is his insistence that these organizations for social good are also run as viable businesses, not charities. That way they have to be both effective and efficient. The *Big Issue* is now fifteen years old and has been profitable for eight or nine of them, having suffered, like every publication, from a dip in advertising in the early years of this decade.

'What is interesting,' says Gordon, 'is that where it went adrift it was partially because they forgot that the major focus always, always, had to be the people who sell the papers. The whole business exists for them.' That is the distinguishing difference in a social business. It works for the clients, not the owners. 'It is such a wonderful business,' Gordon says, 'because everyone said it was not possible. They said these people were lazy and drunk, they will never work. But they do.'

Then there is the cooperative that Gordon has been instrumental in helping the Kayapo Indians of Brazil to set up to sell their products more profitably and make their future more secure. He first became involved in Brazil in 1987 when he established the nut oil business for the Body Shop. This led to the Body Shop Foundation setting up and largely financing the Xingu Project, providing health and education for the indigenous peoples, who had suffered hugely from their exposure to first world infections. Since 1998 Gordon has acted as adviser to the cooperative as well as providing start-up funds.

He has now created the Amazonian Rainforest Foundation to help the seven tribes in the area to secure their own lands and to become more self-sufficient, although he admits that the long-term future for these indigenous people is not bright. The pot in his still life was given to him by the Assurini, one of the tribes in the region whose survival is now very fragile. Their numbers had dropped to only sixty-five because they had stopped having children, traumatized by their treatment by white people. The population has climbed back to 103, but its future, like all Amazonian tribes, is very uncertain.

Another of Gordon's social business interests is Freeplay. Inventor Trevor Baylis had created the wind-up radio but failed to find a company to take up his invention and manufacture it, despite its obvious advantages for the developing world where electricity is

They ran a small hotel together, a picture framing business and a restaurant, and then came the Body Shop. 'Anita took care of all the creative and interesting parts while I took care of the contractual and finance parts, which I thought were the interesting bits, and it grew and grew and grew, and we loved it all. We also thought of it as a political gadfly and used our windows to promote our causes. Yes,' he says, 'I was always imbued with a sense of outrage whenever I saw injustice or people being treated unfairly.'

Gordon grew up in a Presbyterian egalitarian culture in Scotland, his father having died when he was four. The clock in the still life was in the family home in Aberdeenshire and remains a symbol of family life, as does a jukebox that still stands in his kitchen today. The Presbyterian culture never took hold of him, however. His preference, if anything, was always for the Eastern religions while wine instead of water, particularly Pinot Noir, soon became his drink of choice. Today there is a vineyard and a winery in his garden that produce a very passable champagne-type wine and he has only recently sold a chain of small hotels called Hotel du Vin. Books, too, feed his life and he intends to write a book for his grandchildren, being as truthful as he dares, but one suspects that there are many more social businesses and social concerns to fill his time before he gets round to that.

His enthusiasm for remedying some of the wrongs of the world is infectious, but he seems to have discovered how to make the most of his time and energy by staying close to, but at one remove from, the organizations that can deliver some of those enthusiasms. For a man who started out with no ambition except to ride a horse and enjoy life, he has travelled far and, perhaps, has found more enjoyment along the way than he could have expected. Righting injustice and helping those less fortunate than oneself is, as many have discovered, good news for both the helper and the helped.

## *Still Life*

Riding boots – horses, polo and the American ride
Belu water – social businesses
Assurini pot – the fragility of life, particularly in the Amazon
Wine book – wine and books
Clock – love of family and home
Rose in a Body Shop bottle – Anita and the Body Shop

# David Ross

D avid Ross has always liked a challenge. If it isn't presented to him, he will create one. He will also make sure that he succeeds. 'I like to do things properly,' he says. And by properly he means as well as anyone could. 'David always aims high,' said his partner Shelley, who knows him better than most. His latest self-imposed challenge – building an opera house in the stableyard of his country house as the home for a summer opera festival – might strike some people as a challenge too far for someone who is not yet forty years old, and still in the midst of a demanding business career. But not too far for David Ross. 'Having rescued this beautiful place,' he says, referring to Nevill Holt in Leicestershire, the pre-Tudor mansion he has transformed from an old preparatory school into the grand house and gardens that it is today, 'I wanted to find a way to let others enjoy what it has to offer.' How he became, among many other things, an innovative patron of the arts and a philanthropist so early in his life is an intriguing story.

David was born in Grimsby, where his grandfather had founded Ross Foods. Business was in his blood 'Since the age of thirteen I have always wanted to be involved in an entrepreneurial business,' he says. He went to school at Uppingham, an independent boarding school, where he met Charles Dunstone. The friendship that they formed there was to lead to greater things when they joined forces to create Carphone Warehouse, one of the most successful businesses in Britain in the 1990s and still expanding.

But those heady days were still in the future. David first went to Nottingham University to study law and then joined Arthur Andersen to train as an accountant, where he learnt the essential disciplines of a good business. When he moved over to the insolvency side of the firm and saw what happened when those disciplines were missing it sharpened his ambition to be an entrepreneur. It was there that he met Simon Freakley, his immediate boss, someone who would continue to be important to him later on.

He had been at Andersen for eighteen months when Dunstone reappeared in his life. Dunstone had started working at NEC in its mobile phone business, selling, in those early days, mainly to corporate clients. Dunstone could see a different future, one in which the mobile phone would begin to replace the landline. At the time the general public was ignorant and suspicious, and the then Chancellor, Norman Lamont, wanted to tax these 'yuppie accessories'. Dunstone opened a small shop, offering 'simple, impartial advice from experts', and invited his old friend to join him. Ross saw an entrepreneurial opportunity and needed little persuasion, although Simon Freakley was somewhat surprised when he offered his resignation. 'I don't think he had heard of anyone leaving Andersen to work in a corner shop before.' Ironically, it was Andersen that was to disappear, while Carphone Warehouse has flourished.

David Ross became deputy chairman, in charge of strategy, a post he still holds and to which he gives about one third of his time. In 1991 Nokia entered the market with the first hand-held device. Then came new operators such as Orange and Cellnet and the industry took off. The small company the two friends had created was now trying to keep pace, opening outlets in every major high street, but it was the purchase of Tandy in 1998 with its network of stores that transformed its business. Today the company has more than 500 stores in the UK and 700 overseas. It has recently added a cheap-rate fixed line service to its offerings, a logical diversification and one that provides another growth opportunity, helped by the deregulation of fixed line systems in Europe. In 2000 the company was floated on the London Stock Exchange, valued at £1.7 billion. David Ross, with a twenty-five per cent share, was rich, at least on paper.

In the meantime his success was being watched. His skills and experience were sought after in a wide variety of fields. He joined the boards of National Express where he is now chairman, then the Big Yellow Group and Trinity Mirror. ('All of them in interesting industries that were new to me,' he comments.) As if he needed yet another business challenge he has recently begun to buy a range of shopping centres in the States.

The English Sports Council recruited him to its main board as did the Wembley National Stadium – both of them are facing difficult challenges, just what David Ross seems to thrive on. But perhaps the most fascinating assignment was the invitation to become a non-executive director of the Home Office Audit Board, with a brief to cast his eye over its many operations, including, recently, the immigration process at Heathrow Airport and his local prison at Market Harborough in Leicestershire. He is full of praise for the Home Office in its willingness to throw open its workings to outsiders such as himself. And it is, David reflects, very satisfying to find that his skills and experience are of value to the wider community.

He is, rather obviously, a busy man although he gives the impression of unhurried calm. The secret is communication, he says, with all his varied communities, something, of course, for which the products of Carphone Warehouse are designed. Watchful delegation is also key, one suspects, because he does not have a big personal staff. 'I don't really feel I'm working,' he says. 'These are just the things I do, the things I enjoy.'

He also has to find the time for the challenges of his private life. He is an outdoor man and likes to set himself demanding physical tasks – climbing Mount Kilimanjaro or Mont Blanc, running a marathon or cycling the length of France with a group of Carphone

# Peter Ryan

P eter Ryan is proof that you don't need to be mega-rich to make a difference as a philanthropist. He left his job as the manager of a French food company and set up the MicroLoan Foundation, which now provides micro-loans to the women of Malawi to help them to get started in business. He asked Bob Geldof to be its patron, and Bob agreed. Peter put in around £25,000 of his own money to pump-prime it, but is now looking for funds from friends and interested people as well as from the Department of International Development. More crucially, he gives the founda-tion almost half of his working time, two to three days a week, supervising it all from his home in London.

It started small in Malawi. 'At first we employed a local man who had experience of lending, equipped him with a bicycle and sent him off to start a couple of pilot groups to see how things panned out. Then I came back home to Chiswick to raise money to pay for his modest expenses and more start-up capital for loans. The first talk I gave I raised £150 and went on for about fifteen minutes too long and the makeshift screen provided by the church tumbled down halfway through. Like all human undertakings it was far from perfect but we were away . . . it does not take much to take that first step,' he says.

'That first man on a bicycle is now our programme director with a smart four-by-four vehicle. There are twelve loan officers with motorbikes, an operations director, an administrator, an accountant and two book-keepers. They have made over 6,000 loans, supporting around 30,000 dependants, of whom around 6,000 are children orphaned by AIDS.' Peter hopes to be making 20,000 loans a year before too long, out of 15 or so loan offices around the country, helping to support some 100,000 people, 20,000 of them AIDS orphans. He is currently putting together a business arm of the charity, called Microventures Trading Ltd, which will manage specialist business skills training such as vegetable growing, knitting, sewing and paper-making and be able to sell Fairtrade products. In time he would like to move into other countries in sub-Saharan Africa. The foundation is coordinated by a small group or people in London who give their time for free.

The loans are truly micro – typically between 6,000 and 12,000 kwatcha, about £25 – £50, but serious money in a Malawian village. They are given to groups of women, because it is the women who shoulder all the day-to-day economic responsibilities of providing for the family. Loans last for just four months, after which ninety-seven per cent of the money will have been repaid, with interest. It's a tight timetable, but Peter's business experience has taught him that no business ever failed because it had been pushed too hard in its early days. The interest element is also important, Peter feels, partly because the women need to know that you cannot borrow money for free, but also because the interest payments should in due course cover the local operating costs so that the whole enter-prise will be self-sustaining in the longer term.

Before the groups get their money they have to attend training sessions over a six-week period. They learn the basics of book-keeping, cash flow and budgetary control as well as how to struc-ture their group with a chairperson, a secretary and a treasurer. They then have to present a business plan. The foundation's British finance director observes that the groups have to demonstrate far more rigorous business understanding than many people who borrow from UK banks.

The businesses are micro, too. Some women buy goods such as fish, tomatoes or second-hand clothing to sell at market, for example, or they might choose to bake doughnuts or brew beer. The foundation has also financed several budding restaurant owners, or, to be more precise, stalls selling mugs of tea and bowls of maize porridge. One business produces hand-painted greeting cards. Peter says that many of the women respond with astonishing enthusiasm to the training and the discipline, because for some of them it is their first experience of being taught anything. 'Just because people have never been to school,' Peter says, 'does not mean, in our experience, that they are not both staggeringly intelligent and keen to learn. You only have to participate in one of the group question and answer sessions to appreciate that.'

The results are out of all proportion to the input. Typically, after the first loan the women will use their profits to buy food and clothes for their families, which often have up to twelve or fourteen members, including grandmothers and almost invariably a number of children orphaned by AIDS. After a second loan they will probably be able to send their children to secondary school. This costs £5 a term, a derisory sum to us but way beyond the reach of most Malawian women. After a third loan they can invest in a bit of home improvement – a corrugated iron roof, for example, that does not leak. Often, after four loans, they are not only able to build new homes from scratch but, in some instances, are running businesses that employ other people as well. Most crucially, however, they have discovered how to take charge of their own lives, to remove themselves from the trap of dependency.

It's an inspiring story, but it takes some chutzpah to launch such an undertaking. Peter wasn't fazed by it. 'If you are committed to something you just do it, come what may. I have set up a few new businesses in my career and done them quite well, though never for myself, because I have never felt that strongly about any of them and might not have stayed the course. My first job was creating manufacturing contracts for a toiletries company in Africa. Later I set up a business for Duracell across Africa and the Middle East and started a food business in the UK for a large French food company. More recently, I've been involved in setting up some software businesses for the food industry and currently I'm working as managing director of a division of a quoted technology company. I have a track record of putting people together, building networks, combining my marketing and business skills. So I knew I could do it. A lot of it has to do with the vision and with marketing that vision. If you can touch people's hearts, they will get involved.'

How and why did a corporate executive with a wife and two teenage children embark on such a venture in mid-career? The story starts when a friend of Peter's passed through the Philippines on a world tour in 1987 and was struck by the extreme poverty in parts of that country at that time. The friend gave a personal loan of £150 to a family to help them buy goods to sell. He returned a year later, picked up the loan, lent them some more and then to someone else. Next he started a very small foundation. Peter says, 'I supported that charity, with my wife. Then in 1997 I went to see for myself what he was doing. It was then that everything just lit up. I said to myself I've just got to do this, so I created my own charity. The original concept was that we would support my friend's work and grow our charity in the Far East. But after I had sat down and had got Bob Geldof as our patron it became clear that our vision was bigger than my friend's. So we decided to plough our own furrow somewhere else, while still supporting his work in the Philippines.'

He talked to a fundraiser and others back in the UK and it became clear to him that the need and opportunity was in Africa and those contacts led him to Malawi. Peter knew Malawi from his earlier travels in Africa. He knew the need. 'Imagine,' he says, 'if we had to dress our children in the ragged clothes that our UK charity shops reject. If we had to sit by and watch twenty per cent of them die before the age of five. If living to the ripe old age of thirty-eight was a major achievement because it meant that we had exceeded the national life expectancy, and if, in the years when the harvests fail, as they did two years ago, we would have to sit in agonizing

silence and watch members of our family slowly starving to death.'
He recalls going to a Sunday service in a packed church of some
500 worshippers with a couple of choirs and a Sunday school of
200 children. They read out the total of the last week's collection.
It came to less than £10.

The answer, he knew, was work and jobs, but the people would
have to create most of these themselves. Malawi was a relatively
stable society in which he felt that his idea of business training and
loans could make a real difference. If it worked in Malawi, it might
be possible to go on to tackle the tougher countries such as Sudan.
He placed an advertisement for the first loan officer in the largest
national newspaper in Malawi and flew out to interview a shortlist
of thirteen applicants. He was off.

Peter, now in his early fifties, sees this project as defining a large
part of his life for the next twenty years or so. What is there in his
background to explain such a major commitment of his time and,
to some degree, of his money or, more precisely, the loss of the
money he might have made in that time? His home is filled with
Victoriana acquired over the years and, although he wonders whether
he would go out and buy it now, there is a sense in which he is
himself a Victorian. He believes in many of the values of that age
– the importance of the family, church-going, a sense of obligation
to others and self-responsibility – reinforced by his study of Jung's
philosophy. That sense of personal responsibility came early when
his parents' marriage broke up and his father left home. He was
thirteen and had to grow up quickly. That childhood experience
may partly explain the importance he attaches to his own family
and to his local church community, which has actively supported
his Malawi venture. Indeed, it is these underpinnings of support that
probably allow him to make the most of his entrepreneurial and
pioneering instincts. The Victorians, at their best, were a combination of duty and enterprise.

These old-fashioned values have in the past come into conflict with
his business instincts. He tells how once, on a family holiday in Thailand,
he bought a souvenir doll from an old woman in a market who was
clearly very poor. He bargained the price down and down until he
was quietly satisfied with what he terms his capitalist achievement.

'Every time I look at that doll now I see the face of that poor old woman and am ashamed. I have paid for that doll a million times more than what I physically paid, because I say to myself, "Peter, how could you do that to that poor woman?"'

You could say that he is still repaying his debt to that woman through his Malawi operations. Peter sees it more straightforwardly: 'It turns me on,' he says. In some ways he is a truly simple man, self-effacing, unheroic, doing what he feels is right and using his skills to make it work. He would always prefer to let his actions speak louder than words. Tellingly, his favourite flower is the tulip, plain but right.

## Still Life

Victorian stool – one source of values
Photograph – the family
Thai doll – conflict of values
Greeting cards – products of a Malawi business
Book by Jung – self-understanding
Tulip – simplicity and goodness

# Ricardo Semler

Ricardo Semler is famous in the business world for his revolutionary approach to managing his company Semco based in São Paulo, Brazil. He lets his employees set their own hours, wages and even create new areas of business for the company and share in the resulting profits. Now, after twenty-five years of proven success in his business, he is applying the same philosophy to two new schools that he has established in the city, one private, one public. He hopes that his methods will result in young people taking more responsibility for their lives and their work in the future.

His philosophy emerged from near disaster. Fresh from law school, at twenty-one he took over his father's smallish business, which manufactured pumps and propellers for the world's merchant marine fleets. Eager to prove himself, he worked sixteen hour days, jumping on planes to raise capital to expand the company, until he collapsed on the floor of a factory he was visiting. The doctors warned him that if he continued to work at this pace he would have a heart attack. He came home resolved to change the way he worked but also, and as importantly, the way his employees worked.

Ricardo decided to trust his workers to take on more responsibility for how and when they worked. He cut the central staff by seventy-five per cent to just fourteen people and the layers of management from eleven to three. 'It's no good contacting the centre,' he told his workers, 'there won't be anyone there.' The workers also decide between themselves in each unit how to divide the profit-sharing bonuses. They have unrestricted access to all corporate records and are taught how to read financial reports. They set their own wages and their own production quotas, they hire and fire their fellow workers and they vote on all major decisions. There is no dress code but there is one firm rule – that they take their holidays. Give people the freedom to do what they want, says Ricardo, and over the long haul their successes will outnumber their failures. 'It seems,' he says, 'that if you trust people to do the right thing and it's in their interest to do so, then they will do their best to make it happen. We treat our people as adults, not adolescents.' It is, you might think, only common sense.

But does it work? After all, although other business leaders queue up to visit Semco to see how it works, none of them have copied it. Well, after ten years of this philosophy, productivity at Semco had increased sevenfold and profits had risen fivefold in spite of the chaotic economics of Brazil at that time. Today the firm is growing by itself with partner companies around the world, a policy that allows the people in Brazil to keep learning and to be in touch with what is happening in the rest of the world. The numbers employed directly by Semco have grown from a few hundred at the start to over 3,500 today, while profits have risen from $35 million to $212 million in the last 6 years. It is now its twelfth year of twenty-seven per cent growth. But growth does bring problems. To maintain the same level of communication with the workforce Semco has had to create the equivalent of its own union to be the trustee or guardian of the culture.

So, yes, Semco works. But, Ricardo asked himself, does he, now in his mid-forties, want to go on doing the same thing for the next forty years? He was walking in Mount Auburn Cemetery in Cambridge,

Massachusetts, a few years back. It is, he says, a beautiful place, perfect for reflecting on life and death, and he got to thinking about how he wanted to be remembered. Or, more interestingly, why he wanted to be remembered at all. He came away from that walk resolved to create something that would exist independently of him.

The first thing he set up was what he called the DNA Think Tank, to look at the DNA of Brazil fifty years hence. He identified fifty people who were the thought leaders in fifty different fields and brought them together once a year for three days to consider the Gordian knots of Brazil's future, to puzzle out how to cut those knots and to examine the assumptions that they had brought with them. 'I wasn't the chairman or anything and now people don't remember that I had anything to do with it.' He put in $2 million to get it going but it is now self-supporting, backed by nine large businesses. As in all his ventures, responsibility was vested in those involved. In this case they were top-level thinkers. His next venture would be completely different.

In 2003 he started his first school, after two years spent trying to decide what it is that we as a tribe want our children to know before we send them out into the world. And when do they need to learn these things? What would happen if, as well as treating the Semco workers as adults not adolescents, one also treated young kids as adults? Hundreds of parents were interested in the idea but only six sent their children first time round. 'Now we have 100 kids,' he comments. 'Then we took over a second school with 300 pupils, of which 200 were publicly funded, up to 18 years old. We had nine offers to take over public schools so there is some interest there, but we are not interested in growth for its own sake. We don't think we can guarantee quality at that speed of growth.'

As in Semco, the pupils, some of them as young as two, decide whether or not to go to class. They can sit and watch videos or play computer games if they choose. In the end, it seems, they decide that they don't want to miss out on what all the others are doing, so they join in the classes. But it takes time, and patience from the teachers. The children discipline each other in their assembly, and participate in the decisions about the school along with the teachers.

They can, says Ricardo, exhibit astonishing maturity in their decisions, dealing sensitively but toughly with disruptive members.

Why a school in the first place? 'Because we found that the people who came to work for us in Semco had been hammered into submission by the education system. They only wanted to follow orders. When we looked at the problems we were having it was obvious that they had started at two years old.' That, then, was where they would have to start to rectify the problem. It would be easier in the end than re-educating the adults. It is early days, too soon to know whether it will produce the results that Ricardo hopes for, but now that other schools have expressed interest the hope is that after a few years the state school system will adopt some version of the method. That will also lift some of the burden on his own time and money.

Ricardo currently gives the school projects some 20 per cent of his time and is the only funder. It costs him about $150,000 a month, which includes paying for the seventeen researchers in an institute attached to two universities, who are studying and registering every moment of what is happening, because, he says, it has to be properly monitored and repeatable if it is to be a model for others. About 40 per cent of the school expenses are paid by fees, the rest falls to him alone. 'No one else gives a cent.'

Then there is his botanical garden project, which is also eating up much of his money at present. He is creating a botanical garden in partnership with Britain's Eden Project, having bought the land and donated it to a foundation. The garden is situated in a 26-square-mile area around a small village about two hours' drive from São Paulo. He sees it as part of a community regeneration project, based again on his policy of trusting the people themselves to get it right with the minimum of help. 'I am trying to prove that in a third-world situation you can develop a first-world quality of life without it having to do with money, by a change in mentality only.' The project started with the children in the local school, then when the parents saw what their children were learning, they asked for more education too. Now eighteen per cent of the parents are in school.

He has started a programme in the village to develop community leaders, in the hope that they would begin to deal with the alcohol and drug problems that were rife in the community. The botanical garden offers jobs, and he is developing a revolutionary boutique hotel, to be designed totally around the needs of the guests, in the middle of the botanical garden, which will also create jobs. 'I offered it to a group of sixteen businessmen as an interesting experiment for them to invest in that would probably lose money. Twelve of them accepted!' Other activities have begun to spring up around these ventures and the drug problem 'simply went away'. Unemployment in the community has fallen from thirty-six per cent to three per cent. 'We also have a little centre that helps the locals to change their life – if they want to – finding distributors in the city for their products, for example.'

Into this mini-world he feeds other experiments, bringing, for instance, 100 teenagers from all over, some from rich backgrounds, some from poor, to live together for a few days in self-sufficiency. Why? 'We don't know what will come from it but they are meeting up with kids from completely different backgrounds, and they are at least learning about other worlds.'

So that's more money going out? 'Yes. But I enjoy making money, and spending it, so that's no sacrifice. I want to leave the net result constant, putting back as much as I make. I'm no good at running things,' he says, 'I'm a poet. I believe in the unlikely. Some of them are probably pipe dreams but I believe in them. It doesn't matter if no one else believes in them. I'm not doing anyone any harm.' He hopes that some of his projects may be models for the future and may, one day, be self-sustaining. If not, at least he will have tried.

What sort of philosophy drives this unusual man? Some of the clues lie in the objects he chose for his still life, such as the stuffed animal belonging to his young son. It is a memento of his child, but it also warns him not to grow up too quickly. 'Kids make you look at things differently. As we grow older the childish things become more important once again. In the middle of life things get too serious and you miss out on a lot of fun. That's why the work with the schools is so interesting.' At heart, however, he is a social experimenter, but, like good experimenters, he knows that if it doesn't work, it can be changed – like the pencil that's there, too, he comments, he is only making temporary marks on life; all can be erased.

So Ricardo keeps a notepad by his side to note down the flood of ideas that come to him. Eighteen or twenty a day, he says, make it on to that notepad. The good ones generate an email to someone to do something, for he also knows that things work better if he manages his experiments by remote control, because 'my presence is chaotic. I am a destabilizer.' But to balance this restless creativity he needs his music. 'Music takes me into the world of emotional intelligence and affection. It balances my need for rationality.' He plays the guitar and, more recently, the cello. It is, he has discovered, a new challenge to learn to do something that he doesn't do well and at which he knows he won't excel. Unlike much of the rest of his life there is no particular goal here. It is just something to be done for its own sake.

It is the sunflower that perhaps sums him up best, however. 'Like the sunflower, my head gets turned all the time to the light and the warmth, and that light constantly comes from a different direction, so you have to keep twisting your neck. You have to keep flexible.' His father, he recalls, was very different. He did the same thing at the same point every day. To Ricardo it is a terrible waste of this short amount of time that is given to us on this earth not to try to figure out how things are and how they could be. 'Of course, you end up making a lot of mistakes, but they don't usually matter.' A man of ideas, then, always turning to any light that might just make things and people work a little better. A man who knows from his own experience how to get those ideas translated into action. He is indeed an entrepreneurial philanthropist.

## Still Life

Stuffed animal – childish fun
Pencil – anything can be changed
Notepad – ideas
Music sheet – emotional intelligence
Remote control – keep a distance
Sunflower – light and flexibility

# Jeff Skoll

When Jeff Skoll was fourteen his businessman father came home one day with the news that he had been diagnosed with terminal cancer. What Jeff remembers from that evening is his father's regret, not that he would die, but that he had not done all the things he wanted to do in life. Jeff resolved that he was not going to make the same mistake. Luckily, he already knew what he wanted to do, and no, it wasn't to run something like eBay, the internet auction company that he and Pierre Omidyar were to start some years later. He wanted to write stories, stories with a purpose. Even then his dream was to do his bit to make the world a better place. Today his stories take another form but the dream lives on. It has become the driving focus of his life.

As a lonely kid on an island in Canada where the family spent their vacations he had immersed himself in all the books he could find in the house, including, importantly perhaps, the works of Ayn Rand. The world, he could see, was an interconnected and troubled place, with many problems, dangers and injustices. He sensed that by the time he grew up, and maybe had kids of his own, the world was going to be a less pleasant place. So, if these books had had such an effect on him, then perhaps he too could write stories, stories that would alert people to what was going on and maybe spur them to take action.

But he was a realist. He would also need to make a living and he knew that he could not rely on writing to survive. That set him off on an entrepreneurial path, starting with a degree in electrical engineering from Toronto University that should, he reckoned, be a useful base for a business career. But he was in a hurry. Jobs in organizations would not give him financial independence soon enough to enable him to start writing. He would have to do it on his own. 'If you have a big vision, you can't get to it incrementally,' he says. 'You have to take risks. My classmates thought I was crazy, but I have always done the opposite to the conventional. I will go vertical when others go horizontal. It's the entrepreneurial instinct, I guess.' This spirit was not too common in Canada then, though in later years he was to create the Leaf Initiative as a way to promote a more entrepreneurial culture in his home country.

He started his own consulting business, quite brazenly learning as he went along, and then a computer rental company, only to realize that his business skills needed some polishing if he was going to achieve anything big. An MBA from Stanford would do nicely, but he had first to prove to the business school that he had the finances to see him through. He didn't. But, ever the entrepreneur, he persuaded a friend to lend him the money for a day, just long enough for him to show his greatly improved bank statement to the authorities.

It was at Stanford that he met Pierre Omidyar, a very bright computer scientist who was working for a company called General Magic, which developed the predecessors of today's hand-held personal digital assistants like the BlackBerry. Pierre approached him with the idea of persuading people to buy and sell things via the internet. Flush with the newly acquired insights of the business school, Jeff said, 'Pierre, that's a really stupid idea.' After all, no one was selling or buying anything online at that time.

So Pierre went off and started to work on his idea while Jeff joined a newspaper group with the remit to put its papers online. But when he approached those in charge of classified advertising, the most obvious newspaper content to put online, he met a resolute resistance to entrusting the most profitable part of the business to the internet. 'So I rang up Pierre and said "Let's do this".' It was suddenly clear to him that here was a vertical opportunity in a horizontal world. As so often, what later seems obvious to all was rejected as crazy at first.

In 1996, at the age of thirty-one, Jeff joined Pierre at eBay. He was responsible for managing the company, while Pierre developed the product and the systems. eBay worked, says Jeff, because it was based on trust and transparency. Jeff believes that people are fundamentally good and will behave well if they are allowed and encouraged to do so. This belief is a fundamental part of his philosophy of life, and eBay enabled him to put it to the test. He was always mindful of his early reading of Ayn Rand and her belief in enlightened self-interest as the motivating force for human endeavour. eBay was based on this principle. It was not, therefore, like other companies. It was led by its customers in a real democracy. Everyone had an equal voice, something that was to frustrate managers used to more conventional organizations where those at the centre did what they thought best.

The principles worked, dramatically: eBay became the fastest growing company in history at that time, the first to reach $1 billion in revenues in under four years. It now has 150 million users worldwide. More than that it was a social invention, allowing anyone anywhere to trade directly with other individuals without intermediaries. It built relationships based on mutual interest. It offered meaningful contacts to the disabled and the bedridden, to single mothers and the lonely, allowing them to make a living, to be respected and to belong to a community. For the first two years Pierre and Jeff ran it themselves, paying themselves nothing, working 100-hour weeks and living, says, Jeff, off leftover food from their friends. Jeff, however, never saw himself as a manager. As the business grew, they brought in Meg Whitman, a talented manager with a background in more traditional organizations, who has run eBay ever since.

In 1998 the company went public. Jeff now had more money than he could have dreamt of. It was time to move on, time to write his stories. He finally left two years later, feeling sure by then that the values they had started with were now built into the culture. Few could understand how he could want to leave the world's most successful company just when it had reached take-off but Jeff was still focused on his original life plan. 'The company was not my dream,' he insisted, 'but the means to enable my dream.' But first he had set up the eBay Foundation with pre-IPO shares that suddenly became hugely valuable when the company went public, a device he has since recommended to other entrepreneurs. It was his first step into philanthropy. Next came his own foundation, the Skoll Foundation, focused on social entrepreneurship.

Social entrepreneurship is a natural blend of Jeff's own entrepreneurial instincts and his urgent desire to do something about the ills of the world by backing some of those working for social change and publicizing their stories. Jeff tells how he was privileged to meet with John Gardner just before he died. John Gardner was the former president of the Carnegie Corporation and the architect of Lyndon Johnson's Great Society programme as the US Secretary of Health, Education and Welfare. Jeff asked Gardner what he felt was the most important thing that could be done to ensure a brighter future for all. Gardner thought about it for a second and then said, 'Bet on good people doing good things.' That is exactly what the Skoll Foundation sets out to do, with Jeff's active involvement. It seeks out, invests in and celebrates outstanding social entrepreneurs from around the world, and supports and connects them through Social Edge, the online community. Most importantly, in Jeff's mind, the foundation celebrates these extraordinary people in its award schemes and at the annual world conference at the Skoll Centre in Oxford University.

Yet Jeff still had his own stories to write, the stories that would alert the prosperous and the influential to the problems of the world. Wealth, however, brings other preoccupations and responsibilities. The foundation demanded his attention, as did the necessity to manage his wealth and the high profile that his success had inevitably created for him. He had no time for the stories, nor, maybe, he felt, the talent to write them. He was, he says, rather depressed. After a few months of confusion he had something of an epiphany. It wasn't, he realized, the actual writing that mattered but what was written, the message. Why not, he asked himself, hire others to do it for him? And why not turn the stories into films, so that they would be seen by more people, make more of an impact?

He had himself been influenced by great films that had high-lighted social injustice or told stories of people who had dedicated their lives to righting wrongs, films such as *Gandhi, Schindler's List* or *Erin Brockovich*. If films like these, great stories with great actors, could be combined with a supporting campaign for social action, maybe the world would notice and some would respond. Why weren't there more such films, he wondered? Then serendipity played its part. He sat next to a Hollywood producer at a dinner party, the first time he had encountered anyone from that world. He asked him why there were so few films that focused on social issues. 'Because there is no money for them,' the mogul replied. 'That's when the light came on in my head,' says Jeff. He could do something about that.

So it was that Jeff went to Hollywood to make his stories. 'Of course,' he says, 'I was aware of the Hollywood adage that the surest way to become a millionaire is to start by being a billionaire and go into the movie business, but I'm also a believer in Herm Albright's advice that a positive attitude may not solve all your problems, but it will annoy enough people to make it worth the effort.'

He started with documentaries. *The New Heroes* aired on PBS in early 2005. Hosted by Robert Redford and produced by Malone-Grove Productions, it consists of four one-hour episodes, each episode focusing on three social entrepreneurs from different countries. Jeff's hope is that it will open people's eyes to some of the intractable problems in other parts of the world and to what some unusual men and women are doing about them.

He then moved on to large-scale feature films. Seven were sched-uled for production in 2005. The first was *Syriana*, starring George Clooney. The story is built around the global oil industry, our dependence on it and its history of environmental damage and corruption. Along with the movie Jeff has organized a campaign entitled 'Get Clean', which is about clean energy and the opportunity as well as the responsibility for individuals to do something about it. He has recruited as partners in the campaign the Natural Resources Defense Council, Conservation International and other environmental groups to pick up on the concerns that he hopes the movie will arouse. Stories, he believes, are what connect the head and the heart and when those two connect action will follow.

The second film, *North Country*, starring Charlize Theron and a number of other leading actors, is based on the true story of a female iron-ore miner who was subjected to sexual harassment by the male workers. She sued the company in what turned out to be the largest class-action lawsuit in the States at that time. This is a movie about female empowerment throughout the world, and again there is an alliance of campaigning groups to support the film.

Jeff is CEO of the production company for these films, and is pleased with the progress so far. 'I came into Hollywood with the premise that people are basically good and that they would want to be involved in things that they could be proud of. When I started talking to actors and directors, even to studio heads, I found that every one of them had a project that they had a passion for; maybe it was autistic kids, AIDS orphans, the environment or some other social concern, but the system was not set up to allow them to do it. We have created the excuse for them to be able to do these projects by buying in the support that is needed. We trust that people are going to want to see these films.'

His interest in the power of films then took a new turn. Inspired by a friend who had been working in refugee camps in Palestine, he has arranged for *Gandhi*, starring Ben Kingsley, to be translated into Palestinian Arabic and shown in those camps in the hope that it will show the inhabitants the benefits of non-violence and passive resistance as a means of change. It is, he admits, a step beyond anything he has done so far, and risky, but then all worthwhile philanthropy involves risk.

Jeff's whole life is based on the assumption that people are fundamentally good. Not all people, maybe, and not all good people are good all the time, but as a working hypothesis it functions surprisingly well. Inspired by a social entrepreneur who put orchids in the classrooms of the schools he had created, Jeff now places an orchid on every desk in his office. Beauty, he believes, brings out the best in people. Beauty, and the chance to make a difference. Aged only forty, Jeff Skoll has already made a difference, although, modestly, he might say that it is all a form of enlightened self-interest. He is only doing what he set out to do all those years ago. Few of us are so consistent.

## *Still Life*

eBay – the source of his wealth
Maple leaf – The Leaf Initiative, for entrepreneurship
Ayn Rand – her philosophy of enlightened self-interest
*Gandhi* DVD – films as agents of social change
BlackBerry – keeping in touch
Orchid – beauty and goodness

# Janez Škrabec

---

Janez Škrabec had just left university in Slovenia when the world that he was about to enter collapsed. It was 1991. Yugoslavia was split apart by civil war. Russia was in economic crisis and RIKO, his family firm that had represented most Yugoslavian engineering businesses in Russia, failed, as did many other Russian enterprises. In the fifteen years since then, starting from nothing, Janez has rebuilt the family business in Slovenia, joined forces with a manufacturing firm in Croatia and become known as one of Slovenia's most successful entrepreneurs.

In the midst of all this activity he has still found time to make his own unique contribution to the society and culture of his country, preserving its heritage, encouraging its arts and investing in sport as a way of developing the nation's youth. 'The world does not know what Guggenheim did,' he remarks, 'but they know what he left behind.' He, too, is determined to leave something of significance behind, turning his business experience to other uses. He is

187

forty-two. Time enough, one might think, but Janez has never waited on time. He has made a start already.

He has transformed the centuries-old Škrabec family homestead into a cultural museum in order to preserve the special heritage of the Ribicna Valley and its people. He would like it, in time, to become the heritage centre for the whole of Slovenia, including workshops for children to remind them of where they come from. 'When I was in the States as a young man I visited Williamsburg and realized the importance of history. Our past is our future. We need localization as well as globalization. People want uniqueness. We are unique in Slovenia. We must preserve what is special to us.' Slovenia is already benefiting from its membership of the European Union, but Janez believes it would be a tragedy if its culture were to disappear into a bland composite of European consumerism. He will do his best to see that this does not happen.

Janez's own ancestor, Father Škrabec, a Franciscan monk and nineteenth century ethnographer who established the rules of the modern Slovenian language, is a key figure in the history of the Ribicna Valley. Janez has established the Father Stanislav Škrabec Foundation in his memory to encourage the study of the Slovenian language and the Franciscan tradition. Through his family company, the now reinvented RIKO, he is also an active sponsor of Slovenian arts and artists, as well as of sports, for he believes that, while art fosters imagination and creativity, sport emphasizes self-discipline, patience, determination and the motivation to achieve one's goals, all crucial to the development of Slovenia's young people. They are our future, they need all the help we can give them,' he says.

Determination and motivation were not lacking in Janez as a young man. He had little else at the start of his career, besides his fondness for Russia, his understanding of its culture and the connections that survived from the failed family business. While Russia was still closed to many foreigners at that time, Slovenia was open and more accessible to Westerners, and had the most entrepreneurial outlook of all the former socialist republics. Janez had used his school holidays to work and study in Germany, the US and Britain, and had spent a year in Russia, and he felt that acting as an intermediary between Russia and the West was an opportunity waiting to be exploited. The Russian economic collapse created a temporary niche market that he hurried to fill, helped, he says, by one very good teacher and mentor, who, sadly, died of cancer a couple of years later, leaving the young Janez on his own.

Janez found a company in Russia, called Autovaz, that made Lada cars. It, too, had gone bust in the Russian crisis and had lost all its distribution channels. He offered to sell its cars on commission, which he did in a wide range of countries, from France to China, as well as Slovenia, collecting the money before handing it on to Autovaz, while living off the cash flow. At that time, he says, there was a general demand for Russian cars, so the business flourished. He went on to supply the machines that Autovaz needed to make the cars, taking the specifications and seeking out the best suppliers, most of them in Germany. The next step was to make the machines himself, for which he needed a partner, so he joined up with an engineering company in Croatia. Then the partnership changed tack again, this time making the component parts themselves, as Janez sensed that the market for the machine tools that make the parts would inevitably become satiated. He likes to keep ahead of the curve.

The business has developed, diversified and grown in output but RIKO itself is still small – only 20 engineers, compared with the 50 or so in the Croatian company where there are over 200 people in total. Keeping it small allows Janez to keep it in the family – 'until I am dead I will never go public' – and under his personal control. 'We outsource as much as we can, even accounting.' He had realized early on that he was essentially in the project management business, connecting and overseeing the work of others, backed up by strategic partnerships. That provides scope for almost infinite possibilities. He was anticipating the way that many businesses would move in the future, becoming the organizing hub of a complex alliance of specialized organizations, focused on particular projects. For Janez it was just common sense. His company is now built around a small and changing collection of major projects.

RIKO is currently project managing the construction of a large hotel in Moscow. To extend its range it has also formed a partnership with Maz, a large producer of trucks in Belarus, and, on the supply side, a cooperation with Kongsberg, a Norwegian company specializing in information technology. Then there is the pioneering venture in eco-housing, where the techniques of metalworking have been adapted to the manufacture of custom-built, solid wooden houses. These are increasingly popular in Slovenia and surrounding countries because of their environmental appeal. Recently, along with his wife Sonia, a professor of sport but as entrepreneurial as Janez himself, he has moved into the health business, constructing a state-of-the-art fitness centre in the capital, Ljubljana. 'Well-being is good business,' he says, good in every sense.

The long-term future of the business is something he won't speculate upon. 'I go with the flow. Everything is uncertain. Tomorrow everything could go.' Like most entrepreneurs he enjoys the uncertainty, which, to Janez, is opportunity. But, he admits, entrepreneurship conjures up the wrong image – of money-making for its own sake, of selfishness and greed. He is proud of the fact that he is better known in Slovenia for the village museum and his philanthropy than for his businesses, with the exception of the wooden houses, which have caught the public's attention. Yet his business and his philanthropy, he insists, are not two separate things. 'I like to integrate our culture into my business, and my philanthropy must be connected with my business, because it is the business that finances it.' When his Russian clients come to Slovenia he entertains them at the museum. 'Then they trust me. They know that I belong here, that I am not going to run off to the Cayman Islands with their money. And business, you know, is built on trust.'

Russia will always be important, not just for his business, but for him personally. He fell in love with the country when he lived there for a year as a young man. 'Russia is my hobby,' he says, 'I love its people.' He keeps the enamel box in his still life on his desk as a memento of his love for the country. 'When I am on the telephone arguing with someone about something, I look at this cute box and it calms me down.' It keeps him earthed. The egg, too, is Russian and was given to him by a Russian Orthodox priest. He is a Catholic himself, believing, he says, that 'I need to give credit to someone for giving me the chance to be successful, credit to the people, credit to the nation, but also credit to God. The Bible is for me very important. It is a book of wisdom. I was impressed by the story of King Solomon. When God asked Solomon what he could do for him, Solomon replied that he would like to have wisdom and heart.' Both are needed, he believes, in business as well as in life.

Russia may be his hobby but his life is rooted in Slovenia, symbolized by the peony, a very typical Slovenian flower, and also by the designer vodka glasses and the wooden spoon, an example of the traditional craftsmanship of the local area. Janez is anxious to promote the arts, both old and new, as well as artists, as being one way to preserve the country's uniqueness, its essence. In front of the entrance to the restored homestead that houses the museum are sculptured columns made by four Slovenian artists, and more of their work is inside. The columns make the point that the new and the old can live together, indeed have to be bonded together to preserve the country's identity. They are a visible testimony to what Janez stands for, linking past and future.

Janez is a businessman and an entrepreneur. He clearly enjoys the deals and the design of the projects he is involved with. And, very obviously, he is good at it. But, as the objects he chose for his still life indicate, business is not the great project of his life. That is Slovenia, its history, language, culture and, crucially, its future. That future will be delivered by the next generation. They are the ones whom Janez really wants to interest in his projects. The businesses, while worthwhile in themselves, service his cause.

Just visible in his still life are a pair of cuff links, a gift from his wife. 'I love my wife very much. She was the first person I ever wanted to marry. I did so as early as I could, when I was just twenty. She is very independent and I appreciate that very much. She would never rely on me.' Janez would not want it any other way. He is, by any measures, a successful, contented man in the prime of his life with much to offer his country and his people.

## *Still Life*

Enamel box – Russia and calm
Russian egg – Russia and religion's wisdom
Wooden spoon – Slovenian craftwork
Vodka glasses – Slovenian design
Cuff links – love and marriage
Peony – beauty and Slovenia

# John Studzinski

John Studzinski is a man of many parts. He uses the example of a Wellington chest that stands in his bedroom to describe his life. It has eight drawers, representing the different aspects of his life, although, as he says, 'one of the drawers is partly closed, which is the private part of me, while another is closed possibly even to myself. I bought it twenty years ago when I came to England. It's stylish but practical – I don't like things that are frivolous or foolish – and it's organized. At present my life is planned twelve to twenty months ahead, my banking work, my charitable activities and my personal life.'

Until recently, John was a member of HSBC's Group Management Board and co-head of its investment banking business, before leaving to join private equity firm Blackstone as a senior managing director and member of its executive committee. But he started his working life at Morgan Stanley in 1980 where he stayed for twenty-three years. It was one of the founders of that firm, Junius Morgan, who once said that an investment banker stands at the crossroads of capital between the sources and the users of funds and thus has an important role in society. John believes that investment bankers have always existed in some form or other and will always be needed, because they stand at those crossroads and can be very constructive allocators of resources. 'I don't like the notion that investment bankers don't add value.'

In their own sphere, John believes, philanthropists have the same function, of reallocating resources in society. He insists, however, that philanthropy is about much more than money. 'I am very cynical about money. Money can be a billboard for some people, or a ticket, but it should be only one of those eight drawers. If philanthropy involves giving your time and energy as well as your money, then you really create something new, and you learn something about yourself in the process. I give time as a trustee, I give an enormous amount of time to fundraising, and I also give time personally, as a management and sometimes strategy consultant. I think this is very important in philanthropy. Unless you take time to understand the clients, the recipients, of your philanthropy, you are not in a very good position to allocate the philanthropic resources.'

He is, indeed, extraordinarily generous with his own time and energy, having managed not only to hold one of the most senior roles in international banking but also to be a vice-chair of US-based Human Rights Watch as well as a trustee of the Tate Gallery in London. In recognition of his work for the homeless in London where he has been chairman of Business Action for the Homeless and a trustee of Passage, the London centre for the homeless, he was made a Knight of the Order of St Gregory by Pope John Paul II. He is also a serious patron of the arts, an enthusiast for trees and nature, a generous host and friend to many from all walks of life, a dog-lover and a serious student of religion and the meditative life. Most of all, however, he is a philanthropist at heart, concerned to foster human dignity in every part of life, to give self-confidence to the insecure and self-esteem to the vulnerable.

The entrepreneurial side of John's philanthropic work is largely centred on the Genesis Foundation, which he set up in 2001 and funds with his own money to the tune of some £1.5 million a year. Genesis supports young artists: it has helped composers of new operas at the Almeida, writers at the Royal Court and young directors at the Young Vic. Despite his reservations about money, it is John's earnings from banking that fund the creative output of these artists.

The early origins of Genesis began in a conversation. 'I was told by a friend that there were people applying to LAMDA, the drama school, who would be perfectly good actors but couldn't afford to go there,' John recalls. 'It would be terrible, she said, if acting was to be dominated by the upper middle classes. So I thought, "Well, that's easy to fix, we can create a scholarship or two, or three." But then I thought that this applies to many more potential artists around the world, people who don't belong to networks, who don't have wealthy parents, who are not sitting in a cultural centre, who may be interested in music, or painting, or poetry. Are there, I asked myself, ways to get those people started and involved?' John's first act of commissioning was a mass for Cardinal Hume's seventy-fifth. birthday by a young composer, Roxanna Panufnik. The success of this commission encouraged him to set up Genesis to give the same opportunity to other artists. 'Young artists are very fragile and insecure. If you can give them their first break, they can evolve with increasing confidence,' he comments.

'If through Genesis we can find one actor or one writer, and if by the end of my life we have created one or two careers that have flourished in the arts, then Genesis will have done something. I do get actively involved myself in selecting these people, but I also believe in using the talents of others, people like David Lan at the Young Vic, Jonathan Reekie at Aldeburgh, Elyse Dodson at the Royal Court, great artistic entrepreneurs in their own right, people who, like investment bankers, also stand between the sources and users of talent.'

It is necessary to go back to his beginnings to understand something of what drives this dedicated man. 'I was brought up as a Catholic in a Polish immigrant family. My mother and father put themselves through school and devoted most of their lives to hard work, good values and education. There was a lot of focus in my early life on music, education, reading, travel. Sleep was not much encouraged. We went to bed at ten and were up at five to practise the piano for an hour or to read a book. There was a great emphasis on achievement. If we got eight As and two Bs, it was the two Bs that got discussed. Time was not something to be wasted. Any spare time had to be used to further one's education or to do something useful. I started cutting the lawn at eleven, and in my early teens I founded the first toll-free hotline in America, called Operation Venus, giving venereal disease information to adolescents. I grew up in a family that didn't have much so I always appreciated the fact that there were other people who had less. It became part of my ethos that part of life had to be giving. From that early experience I also learnt that you can take risks in life if you believe in yourself and the cause.

'In May 1987 I had a near-death experience on the autobahn . . . I felt myself looking down on the scene of the crash below me and later could describe for the court the exact layout of the vehicles . . . the next moment I was down in the back of the car bruised and broken and in pain, someone had decided that I wasn't to die. Since then I have become much more sensitive about the internal side of me. I'm fifty now and I've learnt a lot about myself in the last twenty years, but there is probably still more to come.'

As a result of that experience and his earlier upbringing he is a deeply religious man. But it isn't that simple. 'You could say that I was raised externally as a Catholic, but internally I am a Buddhist.' The Buddha, for John, symbolizes human dignity and self-awareness. 'If I had to devote my life to just one thing, it would be to promoting human dignity.' It was his desire to help adolescents confronting the issues of venereal disease, to bear it with dignity, that inspired his first philanthropic effort; human dignity drives his concern for the homeless; it is at the heart of Human Rights Watch. On his mantelpiece John keeps the sculpture of a small face by Max Ernst that has been used by several organizations to represent the essential dignity of the individual. 'It's a very gentle, innocent face that asserts that every individual matters, that every individual has a right to be treated in a certain way, be it in housing, health or whatever.' It is the essential philosophy that underpins all of John's philanthropy.

His interest in individuals seems to include a wide range of people. 'Yes,' he says, 'I am blessed with an enormous range of friends, whom I treat as family and who include me in their families. Good friendships, like wine, get better with time. I am curious. If I meet someone I find interesting, I must invite them for a meal in the next few weeks, otherwise I will never get around to it. I am conscious, therefore, that I am always building networks, of friends and their families, of business associates, of people in the charity world, networks that will last. The world is a very small place if you are sensitive to networks.'

Although he is a bachelor, he does have a family of his own. 'I love dogs; I have four of them. Dogs give you unconditional love, but the problem is that they are also totally dependent on you, so they force you to be unselfish; the dogs are there and you have to take care of them as well as enjoy their love.' He is passionate about nature, too, and it is a continuing and important strand in his life. 'I have always been fascinated by the simple elements in nature. Even though I love contemporary art and sculpture there is nothing man-made that is better than the sculpture of a great tree. I love trees, I love learning about them and I have a very large collection of trees at my place in New England. The interesting thing about trees, and it goes right back to the Buddha, is that most of the great things they are going to produce will not happen in my lifetime. You have to have a great sense of time if you are going to plant trees. You plant a young tree the same way that you nurture a young artist or help a homeless person, for a great tree like a great artist enriches future generations.'

To combine all these aspects of John's work and interests requires a structured life. Those who know him are constantly amazed at how many spheres of life he engages with, how much he achieves and how many people he can count as his friends. He manages it all with very deliberate care. 'I'm very focused on mind, body and spirit. I pray for twenty minutes every morning and every evening, using my books on religion and meditation. But I also exercise every morning because a healthy body is directly correlated with a healthy mind and spirit. One part of me would love to live a monastic life, but another side is fascinated by making deals, whether in banking or with artists. Then there is a third side of me that is about not abusing what has been given to you. Time is given to you, but so is your body.'

So if he had to sum up how he sees his life and its purpose now? 'I believe that I should try to leave the planet more enriched, spiritually, than I found it. One of the ways you do this is by enriching others, by increasing their self-esteem and enhancing their human dignity, which also enriches you in the process. Which is why I get involved with Human Rights Watch, the homeless, and young, naïve and fragile artists. I'm drawn to fragility, as was St Francis, one of my favourite saints and a champion of the poor. Because I've been given a strong platform in life I feel an obligation to help fragility by sharing some of my strength, not just financial strength but also by encouragement and a positive attitude. I'm not, myself, interested in post-mortem philanthropy. I want to be around to choose the projects and the clients and, if possible, to see some of the results and to be a mentor to some of the recipients, if I can play that role.

'I know there is an early American, possibly New England, bit of wisdom that says, "You had what you spent and you lost what you kept and you have what you gave." All the things in this house don't belong to me, they have been lent to me for my life and I will pass them on, but my investment in other people, all that I have given in terms of time, energy and commitment to others, to building their dignity and self-esteem – no one can ever take that away from me.'

## Still Life

Buddha – core values
St Francis – care for the fragile
Photograph of parents – core values
*The House of Morgan* – banking
Wine bottle – hospitality
CDs – Genesis's support for the arts
Mobile phones, etc. – world of business
Running shoes – health